To My Dear ⋮

With deep gra[titude for all that]
you have brought to my
life through the best
and the worst times of
our lives.

Who would have thought
that such a precious
friendship would have
come out of such an
oppressive experience.

Here's to the many tomorrows
that await our friendship

            Love
               Kathy

                    January, 2001.

The
FRIENDSHIP
BOOK

of Francis Gay

D.C. THOMSON & CO., LTD.
London   Glasgow   Manchester   Dundee

A Thought
For Each Day
In 2001

*Turn your face to the sun
and the shadows fall behind you.*

WHILE SHEEP
SAFELY GRAZE

January

THE hands of time move every day, ticking away the hours and the minutes — indeed, our whole lives are dominated by the clock. Perhaps at no other time do the hands of the clock become so meaningful than at New Year when midnight signifies not just another day passing but the close of the year.

It can be an emotional time, for it is then that the concept of time takes on a new meaning — time to remember, to reflect, even to laugh, perhaps shed a tear or two, as we look back, look forward and wonder what a new year has in store for us. These words by author Minnie Louise Haskins seem appropriate:

"And I said to the man who stood at the gate of the year, 'Give me a light that I may tread safely into the unknown.' And he replied, 'Go out into the darkness and put your hand into the hand of God. That shall be to you better than light and safer than a known way.'"

GO and see your friends often, for weeds grow fast and will all too soon obliterate an unused path.

THE FRIENDSHIP BOOK

<u>WEDNESDAY—JANUARY 3.</u>

ONE of the highlights of the year for the Lady of the House and me is to watch the annual New Year's Day concert from Vienna on television. Coming from the beautiful Golden Hall, there is a feast of lovely Strauss music and ballet dancing performed in front of an audience in festive mood.

By tradition, the flowers which decorate the hall are all scented ones — roses, lilies, carnations and sweet-smelling stocks — given by the people of San Remo in Italy, the City of Sun. As an extra gift, there are bunches of long-stemmed pink roses which are given out amongst the audience during the playing of "Roses From The South".

Perhaps we are not able to give friends flowers on as large a scale as this, yet I'm sure we could give pleasure with even the smallest nosegay. I can't think of a better way to start a new year, can you?

<u>THURSDAY—JANUARY 4.</u>

THE following lines were brought to my attention by a friend. They only take a few moments to read, but don't they just hit the nail on the head?

There is so much good in the worst of us,
And so much bad in the best of us,
That it ill behoves any of us
To find fault with the rest of us!
                    Anon.

FRIDAY—JANUARY 5.

HAVE you ever heard of a 12th-century philosopher called Maimonides? I must confess the name meant little to me until I read an article which quoted some of his thoughts:

"I believe in the future, however distant, when no-one will go hungry; there will be no war, no fanaticism, and no conflict between others; when each nation shall bless each nation and will live in peace."

What a lovely prospect! Unfortunately, this is a situation which is difficult to achieve, but would it not be a wonderful idea to adopt these words as a prayer for this century, giving us new hope for the future?

SATURDAY—JANUARY 6.

THE twelfth day of Christmas, 6th January, the Feast of Epiphany, commemorates the arrival of the Magi, the Three Wise Men from the East, bearing gifts for the baby Jesus.

In Ireland there is a country custom, which celebrates 6th January as "Women's Christmas", when mothers are waited on hand and foot.

What a lovely thread to weave into the tapestry of Christmas!

SUNDAY—JANUARY 7.

HE restoreth my soul: he leadeth me in the paths of righteousness for his name's sake.

Psalms 23:3

THE
JACOBITE

75014

MONDAY—JANUARY 8.

HAVE you a project on hand which is not going as well as it should? Perhaps you are tempted to give up, although you know it is a worthwhile goal to aim for. Well, please don't stop — we all encounter setbacks of one kind or another in life; think positively, say "I can," and you will, I am sure, finish your project successfully.

An encouraging thought to keep in mind is these words from Rev. C. H. Spurgeon: "By perseverance the snail reached the ark."

TUESDAY—JANUARY 9.

ONE day in the 17th century a young lad shuddered in the icy Winter wind. He must hurry home to his warm, comfortable home in Leeds, he decided. Suddenly, he noticed a poor boy who looked "starved", the local word for being both frozen and hungry. John peeled off his warm coat and placed it on his shoulders.

It proved to be not merely an isolated action from John Harrison, rather the forerunner of hundreds of other acts of kindness in later life. Although wealthy, John Harrison spent most of his money on other people and numerous good causes; he never regretted his generosity.

His lasting memorial is the church he built in his native city. St John the Evangelist, Upper Briggate, in Leeds, is visited by many people today who still recall this man who was such an example to all.

THE FRIENDSHIP BOOK

"**G**RANDMA isn't old," announced the small boy. He had been listening to the grown-ups and was now making his own contribution.

"You must tell her that when you see her again," his mother smiled. "She'll be pleased."

This story reminds me of the wise words: "It isn't how old you are, but how you are old."

If we can all keep within us the spirit of eternal youth, then the passing years won't be a problem. After all, in our modern society, there are no "old" people, only "older" ones!

I much prefer the sound of that, don't you?

ONE day, the Lady of the House and I saw, in the words of the poet W. H. Davies, that "the world had turned to white".

Snow was falling, drifting down, silently and softly, blanketing the world. It reminded us of this traditional description of a snowfall known to both of us from childhood.

"The men o' the east are pykin (plucking) their
  geese,
And sendin' their feathers here away, here
  away."

It was surely a day to enjoy the simple pleasures of Winter — tea by the fire after an hour spent perusing magazines and books, followed by a little letter-writing to friends in the evening with a before-bedtime browse through new plant catalogues, to remind us of sunny days to come.

FRIDAY—JANUARY 12.

AN old story tells how, after Adam and Eve were driven from the Garden of Eden, it began to snow. As Eve wept, an angel assured her that Spring was on its way. To prove it, the angel touched some of the falling flakes, turning them into white flowers — the very first snowdrops.

A lovely story about a lovely flower.

SATURDAY—JANUARY 13.

TWO men who worked together both gave up their office jobs and went to work for a new company where the conditions seemed better. When they met their new manager, the first man asked, "What are the people like who work here?"

"What were your colleagues like in your previous job?" the manager asked in reply.

"Well, they were generally friendly and supportive," the man replied.

"You'll find the people here much the same," the manager told him.

The second man was asked the same question. He replied, "Frankly, I found them to be an unfriendly and complaining lot."

"You'll find the people here much the same," the manager said.

SUNDAY—JANUARY 14.

AND now abideth faith, hope, charity, these three; but the greatest of these is charity.

Corinthians I 13:13

MONDAY—JANUARY 15.

THESE lines under the heading "What kind of member are you?" appeared in a church magazine. It was written with their congregation in mind, but don't you think there's a message in it for us all?

"Some are like watering cans, they pour out kindness, faith and peace.

Some are like wheelbarrows, going no farther than they are pushed.

Some are like balloons, full of hot air and ready to blow up.

Some are like trailers, they have to be pulled.

But some are like a good watch —

Open face, pure gold, quietly busy and full of good works."

TUESDAY—JANUARY 16.

WE all have our own way of relaxing. Some people meditate or do exercises. Some like to swim or walk, while others enjoy painting or playing a musical instrument. Personally, I like to listen to music.

However you enjoy unwinding, don't let anyone dissuade you from using the time to your advantage. Modern life, with all its hustle and bustle, noise and distraction, means that we all need to "switch off" sometimes. As an old song aptly says: "And let the rest of the world go by".

Whenever you are able, do exactly that. Be good to yourself now and then. You deserve it and those around you will reap the benefits, too.

WEDNESDAY—JANUARY 17.

STANDING on tiptoe
And looking ahead,
We try to discover
The path we should tread.
Or looking behind us,
Lamenting the past,
We yearn for the things
Not intended to last.
Postponing the present
With all that it holds,
We miss all the richness
As nature unfolds.
One day at a time
Is as much as we need,
To meet every problem
And try to succeed.

Iris Hesselden.

THURSDAY—JANUARY 18.

HERE are some lessons in patience for us to consider today:

A modern writer, Simeon Strunsky, remarked that at one time a man would spend a week patiently waiting for the next stagecoach; now he is furious if he misses the first section of a revolving door!

A Somerset farmer, watching the traffic rushing past, said, "The trouble is, they've never had to wait for a crop to grow."

As an old Dutch proverb says: "A handful of patience is worth a bushel of brains."

FRIDAY—JANUARY 19.

THE car was on its regular route, picking up members of a local sixty plus club when suddenly, without warning, the engine just cut out! There was plenty of petrol, so that wasn't the problem. A breakdown van had to be called to tow the car to a garage, and obligingly the driver drove via the intended destination so that the stranded travellers wouldn't miss their meeting.

And what was the trouble? A part had burned out. It was tiny, mind you, just a "cog in the wheel" as the saying goes — but how important, all the same. A reminder that if you ever get a day when you feel rather insignificant, of no real importance to anyone, then remember the vital part played by the small part in that car.

We're all special and important in some way, to someone, and we should not forget that.

SATURDAY—JANUARY 20.

I LIKED this sign seen in a London chemist's shop: *We Dispense With Accuracy*. It reminded me of the road sign seen just outside a small town in California:

Precision Instruments Co. 104 yards, 2 feet, 9 inches ahead.

SUNDAY—JANUARY 21.

AND Jesus went forth, and saw a great multitude, and was moved with compassion toward them, and he healed their sick.

Matthew 14:14

GUARDIAN OF
THE GLEN

MONDAY—JANUARY 22.

ON my travels I came across a blessing that was new to me:
God be in our ebbing,
Christ be in our flowing,
Spirit in us loving,
Love on us bestowing.
It's a lovely thought to keep with us throughout the day.

TUESDAY—JANUARY 23.

I NEVER knew Great-Aunt Louisa, but the Lady of the House and I have in our safe-keeping her scrapbooks and diaries. The former are fascinating collections of quotations and magazine cuttings, plus a hundred and one other things which happened to catch Louisa's attention.

She never married, and instead became a writer and illustrator of children's books, a much-loved lady with a delightful sense of humour. In one of her scrapbooks she wrote these words by Charles Dickens, one of her favourite authors:

"I felt an earnest and humble desire and shall do till I die, to increase the stock of harmless cheerfulness."

Louisa has added in her neat handwriting: "A worthwhile ambition, a dash of unforced, friendly cheerfulness makes life lighter, just like some baking powder in a cake."

Beside her words is a little drawing of a smiling face!

WEDNESDAY—JANUARY 24.

THE Lady of the House and I have a friend, Sarah, who has just celebrated her 85th birthday. She often says with a smile, that she is a "January girl," born on the same date as the poet Robert Burns, the 25th of that month.

So we thought that Sarah would appreciate the following lines, which we wrote inside her birthday card one year:

A JANUARY THOUGHT:

By her who in this month is born
No gems save garnets should be worn;
They will ensure her constancy,
True friendship and fidelity.

Three qualities we can surely all aspire to, no matter when our birthday falls!

THURSDAY—JANUARY 25.

THE year 1997 saw many sightings of comet Hale Bopp. When such spectacles appear, it makes us venture out and look up into the night sky to be rewarded by the sight of such a celestial traveller deep in space.

Often on a Winter's night I have looked up at the stars, and surely if there is anything that puts so much into perspective, it is the sight of the heavens, so infinite that it fills us with awe.

These well-loved words perhaps say it all:

When I look into the heavens
Which Thine own fingers framed
Unto the moon and to the stars
Which were by Thee ordained.

FRIDAY—JANUARY 26.

I FOUND this delightful thought for today from the pen of the American writer F. W. Pitt:

"May you have enough happiness to keep you sweet,
Trials to keep you strong, sorrow to keep you human;
Hope to keep you happy, failure to keep you humble;
Success to keep you eager, friends to give you comfort,
Wealth to meet your needs, enthusiasm to look forward;
Faith to banish depression,
And determination enough to make each day better than yesterday."

SATURDAY—JANUARY 27.

WEATHER REPORT

*HERE is weather information
That could really prove worthwhile.
Don't keep Winter in your heart;
Put Summer in your smile.*

J.M. Robertson.

SUNDAY—JANUARY 28.

AND to you who are troubled rest with us, when the Lord Jesus shall be revealed from heaven with his mighty angels.
Thessalonians II 1:7

THE FRIENDSHIP BOOK

MONDAY—JANUARY 29.

A FRIEND read these words in the office of the hill-walking section of an Opportunities In Retirement club in Ayr:

Protect wildlife, plants and trees.
Make no unnecessary noise.
Leave nothing but footprints.
Take away only memories and photos.

How true! Footprints vanish in a day or two, but memories stay with us for years.

TUESDAY—JANUARY 30.

HERE are two thoughts for us to mull over today:

Kindness is a language that the deaf can hear and the blind can read.

No-one gets giddy doing a good turn.

WEDNESDAY—JANUARY 31.

WHEN I look back over the years, I realise I have been fortunate to have had so many friends. Life would not have been the same without them.

Friendships happen quite naturally, whether through work, leisure or someone who simply lives in the same street. Once you have a friend, then you have someone very special. Remember, a friend is someone you can always turn to, as these lines say:

From childhood years and to life's end
Happy are those who share it with a friend.

February

THURSDAY—FEBRUARY 1.

FEBRUARY is not perhaps most people's favourite month. There may be spells of bitterly cold weather and snow and ice, yet it can be a month of pleasant surprises, too.

By Candlemas Day snowdrops are usually out, followed quickly by crocuses, and quite often we may get a real burst of sunshine to warm up the day and tempt us out into the garden — weather which could pass by unnoticed later in the year but is such a bonus in February. Any time now we will be able to have afternoon tea without the light on and every fourth year, if it's a Leap Year, we'll have a whole extra day to enjoy.

Yes, there's a lot to look forward to in February.

FRIDAY—FEBRUARY 2.

MAY time and tide await your coming,
Gently bear your dreams once more,
All your problems fade before you
As the ocean smoothes the shore.
May the ones you love be happy,
Safe in storms and free from care,
And your life be spent serenely
Sailing where the weather's fair.
                    Iris Hesselden.

SATURDAY—FEBRUARY 3.

A LITTLE group of elderly folk I know meet regularly each week. They look forward to being together and have often said that as we get older, it becomes more and more important to keep in touch with friends.

It made me think of Joe who likes to grow unusual plants in his greenhouse. From time to time he brings us one of them and always says, "When you look at this, think of me" — and, of course, we do.

I think, too, of the bookmark which was sent tucked inside a birthday card with this message:

Just a prayerful way
To say you're thought about today.

This bookmark is a constant reminder that you are in someone's thoughts. Yes, it's good to remember — and to be remembered.

SUNDAY—FEBRUARY 4.

SEEK ye the Lord while he may be found, call ye upon him while he is near.

Isaiah 55:6

MONDAY—FEBRUARY 5.

THE philosopher Epictetus, who was born about 50 AD, knew the value of listening to others. He wrote: "Nature gave us one tongue, but two ears, so that we may hear from others twice as much as we say to them."

It's still good advice today.

THURSDAY—FEBRUARY 8.

WHAT a tingle of delight it gives me to spot the first snowdrop — Spring has almost arrived! But there may be many cold days still to come, so how will that delicate little flower stand up to the frost and snow?

Well, there is a scientific explanation, we're told. At early evening the snowdrop's head droops, its petals close and, as it does so, it retains some of the daytime warmth. It continues to hold this heat, even when the night air is at its coldest. In other words, it has its own central heating system.

You know, the "centrally-heated" snowdrop is a bit like a parable of life: we all get hard times on occasion, and it is then that we must recall and hold to ourselves the warmth of blessings that have been . . . and will be ours again, come the dawn of a new day.

FRIDAY—FEBRUARY 9.

TAKE CONTROL

LIFE is like a trolley,
*   Which never will go straight,*
It deviates, gets out of hand,
*   And never seems to wait*
Unless it's being handled
*   With guidance and with care,*
You'll go the wrong direction,
*   If you are unaware.*

Chrissy Greenslade.

TUESDAY—FEBRUARY 6.

"READ me a story, Grandma!" begg
year-old Emma.

Grandma picked up her well-thumb
and began to read some of the famili
from Genesis. Noticing that little En
unusually quiet, Grandma asked, "Wha
think of that?", referring to the stor
appearance of the rainbow after Noah's fl

"I love it," came Emma's response. "Y
know what God is going to do next!"

WEDNESDAY—FEBRUARY 7.

THE Lady of the House and I were
little hemmed in during some ble
weather — perhaps we had just a sugg
Winter blues. Suddenly, the telephone
our friends Charles and Peggy asked if w
like to join them later that week on a
large garden famous for its displays o
colour. It was to be a guided tour lasting
so we would need to wrap up cosily.

We did, and had a splendid day out o
and sunny February day. We enjoyed
company of our friends, and the w
variety of colour in that garden set off b
frosting of snow.

We returned home, our malaise quite
away by fresh air, exercise and the compan
friends. We are already planning another
outing with Charles and Peggy to en
appreciate the beauty of the world in Wint

SATURDAY—FEBRUARY 10.

I HAVE been reading a little Chinese philosophy and I found it simple and most appealing. Perhaps you, too, would like to share some of this — for example, "From caring comes courage."

And this is my favourite:

"The clouds above join and separate,
The breeze in the churchyard leaves and returns.
Life is like that, so why not relax?
Who can stop us from celebrating?"

If we are honest, we know we have much to celebrate and many blessings to count.

SUNDAY—FEBRUARY 11.

BLESSED are they that do his commandments, that they may have right to the tree of life, and may enter in through the gates into the city.

Revelation 22:14

MONDAY—FEBRUARY 12.

BRIDGET DIRRANE was an Irishwoman who lived to the ripe old age of over a century. She told her life story in a little book "A Woman Of Aran" which is full of quiet wisdom. She finished with these words:

"You may ask, what will I leave when I go for good? It won't be riches. What I will leave is the sunshine to the flowers, honey to the bees, the moon above in the heavens for all those in love, and my beloved Aran Islands to the seas."

She could leave no greater riches.

TUESDAY—FEBRUARY 13.

ONE day, I came across the writing of a man called Adam Gordon. He had led a short but eventful life: born in 1833, the son of a retired Indian Army officer, he received a traditional education in England, but showed such a reckless spirit that he was packed off to Australia at the age of 20.

Spending most of his working life with horses, including an eventful career as a steeplechase rider, Gordon hardly seemed the stuff writers are made of, and indeed did not even begin to publish his work until 1864, six years before his death. One of his verses is especially worth remembering:

Life is mostly froth and bubble,
Two things stand like stone,
Kindness in another's trouble,
Courage in your own.

I like that, don't you?

WEDNESDAY—FEBRUARY 14.

I FOUND these words in the autobiography of Annie S. Swan, a popular romantic novelist:

"My own personal belief is simple. I don't know anything about theology. The only theology which seems to be of the slightest use is to be assured that God exists and that He has something for you to do. His is a gospel of love . . . and I have tried to love others even when I did not like them."

What a simple yet profound statement, one worth sharing today.

THURSDAY—FEBRUARY 15.

FULL of enthusiasm, the Lady of the House once entered a cookery competition at the annual village fete but was later undismayed when her bacon quiche failed to win a prize, due to lack of seasoning.

"I'll learn from my mistake, Francis," she said, as she wrote: "Salt and pepper — don't forget!" by the side of the recipe in her cookbook. "It will remind me that outward appearances don't always win prizes — it's what is inside that matters."

FRIDAY—FEBRUARY 16.

THINGS OF WORTH

LORD, Teach me to see Your hand in things
Around me every day.
Help me to be aware of You
Throughout my work and play.
Acknowledging Your beauty in
The velvet sky at night,
In silken-petalled flowers
And in the morning light.
In beauty of a peaceful sea
And glint of early dew,
The outline of a graceful tree
And in the rainbow's hue.
In all the little creatures
That live upon this earth —
Give me, O Lord, a seeing eye
To know the things of worth.

Kathleen Gillum.

SATURDAY—FEBRUARY 17.

SUSAN is the most smiling person I know, and I told her so one day. "Ah, that's because of a habit I developed when cataracts nearly caused a total loss of sight," she replied. "You see, I could make out people's outlines, but not their facial details, and realised I could be offending folk by not recognising them immediately.

"So I made it a habit to go about with a slight smile on my face. Well, it seemed to work. Friends didn't wait for me to speak first as had so often happened previously — they began the conversation. And, you know," she concluded, "I made many new friends as a result, so the whole experience was a blessing in disguise."

This story reminds me of the saying: "a smile is the shortest distance between two people." It breaks down all barriers, it has no age limit and it's free!

SUNDAY—FEBRUARY 18.

FOR the Lord is good; his mercy is everlasting; and his truth endureth to all generations.
Psalms 100:5

MONDAY—FEBRUARY 19.

FEELING low? Think things are never going to improve? Well, take heart from these lines of the writer J. R. R. Tolkien:

Still round the corner there may wait
A new road, or a secret gate.

THE FRIENDSHIP BOOK

TUESDAY—FEBRUARY 20.

I WENT to visit Tom last week, and found him with his young son, Daniel, who was struggling, not very successfully, to assemble a model aeroplane kit.

"Never mind," I commiserated, as I helped with the unsticking of a misplaced propeller. "Now that you've found out where you went wrong, you'll know how to put it right. After all, the person who never made a mistake, never made anything."

"That's certainly true," agreed Tom, "and in more ways than one. When I first left college, I was so full of my own cleverness I believed I was almost perfect. It wasn't until I learned to accept that I could make mistakes, that I also learned to make something even more important than a model aeroplane."

"What was that, Dad?" asked Daniel.

Tom grinned. "Friends," he replied. "And they really are worth making!"

WEDNESDAY—FEBRUARY 21.

FEAR can come in many shapes and forms. It can be positive, such as the fear which urges and reminds us to take care when crossing a busy road.

However, we all have times in our life when we know less positive fear and long for a little comfort and help. At such times, perhaps this thought from my scrapbook will help: "Fear is like any bully — face up to it, and it backs down."

THURSDAY—FEBRUARY 22.

THE Oak Tree Farm Rural Project near Stafford was initiated by parents and some of their friends with children who had learning difficulties. They wanted the children, on leaving school, to have the same freedom of choice for their future as other young people.

Horticulture seemed an obvious choice, and the first step was to find a suitable site. Now it has become a thriving community, with a farm manager who supervises the animals and an assistant worker from social services. Trainees may also work in all the stages of plant cultivation, and both cut and dried flowers are sold.

Each year there is a design competition when the youngsters plan their own garden plot, using surplus plants. Some need a lot of help, some do it entirely on their own — and I'm told it is always a difficult task to judge.

This project provides new skills for those who might otherwise have had difficulty finding their own particular niche. Long may it prosper.

FRIDAY—FEBRUARY 23.

I WAS walking along the street with my friend Arthur when he suddenly gripped my arm and steered me across to the other pavement.

"The sun's shining over here," he twinkled. "I always think we don't need just to look on the bright side, we can walk on it as well!"

Do you wonder that Arthur is one of the most cheerful people I know?

THE TIME OF HIS LIFE

SATURDAY—FEBRUARY 24.

I DROPPED in to exchange a few friendly words with our friend Mary one afternoon in her spotlessly-clean cottage. I caught sight of a new framed thought on her wall above the fireplace:

Yesterday is history
Tomorrow a mystery,
Today is a gift.
That's why it's called the present.

"I look at it every day," explained Mary. "There's no better time to do things and enjoy friends and family than right now!"

SUNDAY—FEBRUARY 25.

F ROM that time Jesus began to preach, and to say, Repent: for the kingdom of heaven is at hand.
                                                    Matthew 4:17

MONDAY—FEBRUARY 26.

I DIDN'T really have the time
To knock upon her door,
To sit and listen while she
Told me tales I'd heard before.
I didn't think I had the time
To step out of my way,
But I'm so glad I made the time
To cheer her lonely day.
                    Olive Beazley-Long.

THE FRIENDSHIP BOOK

TUESDAY—FEBRUARY 27.

OUR friend Phyllis likes reading old books. One day when the Lady of the House and I called, she was looking at "Aesop's Fables".

"Ah," I suggested, "the story of the hare and the tortoise, perhaps?"

"No, I'm reminding myself of the story about two men who had an encounter with a bear," Phyllis replied. She went on to tell me how, when walking together, they had stumbled into the path of a bear. One, very nimble, quickly climbed a tree. The other, older and slower, dropped to the ground and remained very still, believing that a bear would not touch a "dead" body.

The bear came very close, sniffed round his head, detected no movement and went away. The other man then descended from the tree, came up to his companion and asked, "I saw the bear whispering to you — what did he say?"

"Ah, he warned me to beware of alleged friends who desert you in time of need," came the reply.

Aesop, centuries ago, put forward powerful lessons in a very clever way.

WEDNESDAY—FEBRUARY 28.

BEETHOVEN wrote this little prayer when he realised that his deafness could not be cured:

"O God, give me strength to be victorious over myself, for nothing may chain me to this life. O raise me from these dark depths for Thou alone understandest and can inspire me."

His prayer was answered.

March

MARCH OF TIME

LET the bold March winds come racing,
Prepare for Spring ahead!
Forget the drear of Winter,
Look forward now, instead!
Let determination flourish,
Put those plans into practice, too;
There's a whole new world awaiting,
And it holds bright hopes for you!

Elizabeth Gozney.

OUR friend Alan, who is a primary school teacher, showed me one day a copy of some of the amusing things that his young pupils had written when he asked them to write a Letter To God.

Dear God, — Did you really mean the giraffe to look like that, or was it just an accident that he turned out that way?

Norma.

Dear God, — Instead of letting people die and having to make new ones, why don't You just keep the ones You have now?

Jane.

SATURDAY—MARCH 3.

HOW we take each other for granted! Perhaps we should learn from the example of a lady named Mabel. She had lived for years with her younger sister, Doreen. Mabel had retired some time ago but Doreen continued to work.

One afternoon when Doreen arrived home, she found that Mabel had laid the table for tea using the best china which was usually kept for special occasions.

"Expecting company?" asked Doreen.

"Yes, of course," said Mabel.

"Who?" asked Doreen.

"You," replied Mabel.

They both laughed.

"Thank you," said Doreen.

SUNDAY—MARCH 4.

A TIME to weep, and a time to laugh; a time to mourn, and a time to dance.

Ecclesiastes 3:4

MONDAY—MARCH 5.

GEORGE BURNS, the famous American comedian, once said, "You can't help getting older, but you don't have to get old. I see people who, the minute they get to 65, start rehearsing to be old. They practise grunting when they sit down and when they get up, and by the time they get to 70 they've made it — they're now old!"

No wonder he lived to 100 and was young to the end.

TUESDAY—MARCH 6.

ON a weekend break we were sitting in one of our favourite places — the front seat of a coach — travelling through the Lake District. It had been a beautiful day and the evening was delightful, too.

Sitting opposite us, on the edge of the other seat was a young girl, obviously captivated by the scenery. She smiled and started to chat to us. Wilma had come from Canada to explore as much of this country as possible, staying in youth hostels along the way. We remarked how lucky she had been with the weather, but she insisted that she didn't mind our varied climate at all.

"If I don't like the weather," she said, "I wait fifteen minutes and then there's a change!"

What a lovely way of accepting our many showers. We wished her well as she stepped off the bus and watched her striding off with an enormous back-pack. We hoped she would take home to Canada many happy memories.

WEDNESDAY—MARCH 7.

"THEY" have a lot to answer for. "They" are to blame for everything that goes wrong and "they" are the ones who won't lift a finger to put things right. But who are "they"? Rudyard Kipling knew. He wrote:

"All the people like us are We
And everyone else is They."

Let's stop blaming "Them" and see what "We" can do!

THURSDAY—MARCH 8.

I RECEIVED a letter from a friend overseas in which he referred to the fact that for a long time he had been afraid, but not any more, because he had the five Gs going for him:

Guidance — God guides me in everything;
Grace — God does for me what I cannot do for myself;
Guts — just good old-fashioned courage;
Gumption — good old commonsense;
And the greatest of all — God.

FRIDAY—MARCH 9.

DOUBTLESS you can recall how a pearl is formed. It is formed through pain, and patient determination. A tiny grain of sand gets into the oyster's shell, and acts as a painful irritant; try as it may, the oyster cannot get rid of it, so slowly and patiently, and with infinite care, it builds around the grain of sand layer upon layer of a white milky substance that covers each sharp corner and coats every cutting edge.

Gradually . . . slowly . . . a pearl is made. The oyster has learned to turn adversity into something of great worth and beauty.

Does this not remind you of a person who, despite problems, remains both cheerful and determined — such as the partially-sighted person who talks joyfully of "seeing" the mountains. We are uplifted through contact with such people, truly "pearls beyond price".

SATURDAY—MARCH 10.

SOME friends were sitting having afternoon tea while in the room next door the piano tuner was working, hitting each key until he got exactly the right tone.

The conversation got louder and louder and at times everybody seemed to want to speak at once. Eventually, the tuner's work was done and, to test it, he ran his fingers over the keyboard and played a few bars of a Beethoven sonata.

"Hear what happens when they're played at the right time and in the right order," the host said. "Perhaps we should ask him to come and tune us now!"

SUNDAY—MARCH 11.

AND Jesus came and spake unto them, saying, All power is given unto me in heaven and in earth.

Matthew 28:18

MONDAY—MARCH 12.

MOST of us remember Charles Kingsley because of his masterpiece "The Water Babies". This is what he wrote about friendship:

"A blessed thing it is for any man or woman to have a friend, one human soul whom we can trust utterly, who knows the best and worst in us and who loves us in spite of our faults . . . who will give us counsel and reproof in the days of prosperity and will comfort and encourage us in the days of difficulty and sorrow."

THE FRIENDSHIP BOOK

L ACK of fluency in foreign languages can be a barrier when travelling abroad. But there are times when it is just the opposite! Take the experience of our friend, Anne, for example.

She was on holiday in France, and one morning sat down at a pavement café for a coffee. The only other person at the table was an elderly lady, who at once began to chat nineteen to the dozen. Now Anne knows enough French to get by when on holiday, and like so many of us that is as far as her knowledge goes.

She tried to make this known — but without success — while her companion went on talking and talking until the realisation came that she just needed to talk. At last Anne finished her coffee, got up, held out her hand, and with a smile said "au revoir". They parted just like two old friends.

Language was not a barrier; sympathetic companionship is international.

N EVER wait till it's too late
To say a kindly word.
To greet old friends, or make amends
When quarrels have occurred.

Never wait till it's too late
Delay may bring regret,
So make a vow to do it now
Don't wait and then forget.
Dorothy M. Loughran.

THURSDAY—MARCH 15.

A YORKSHIRE reader found this in a church magazine and alongside was the comment: "One is struck again by the simple truth that God knows best."

I asked for health that I might do great things;
I was given infirmity that I might do better
*   things.*
I asked for strength that I might achieve;
I was made weak that I might learn to obey.
I asked for riches that I might be happy;
I was given poverty that I might be wise.
I asked for power and the praise of men;
I was given weakness that I might sense my
*   need of God.*
I asked for all things that I might enjoy life;
I was given life that I might enjoy all things.
I got nothing I asked for but everything I
*   hoped for.*
In spite of myself my prayers were answered.
I am among all men most richly blessed.

FRIDAY—MARCH 16.

WHEN Doris Lessing was a young, struggling writer she received a letter from people she did not know enclosing £100. They wanted to help her succeed.

In return they asked that, when she was able, she should pass on the money to someone else with the request that they do the same.

Perhaps that £100 is still changing hands today, helping others to find their feet . . .

THE FRIENDSHIP BOOK

SATURDAY—MARCH 17.

A N unknown hand wrote our thought for today: "The nature of God is a circle of which the centre is everywhere and the circumference is nowhere."

SUNDAY—MARCH 18.

J ESUS saith unto her, Said I not unto thee, that, if thou wouldest believe, thou shouldest see the glory of God?

John 11:40

MONDAY—MARCH 19.

L ISTENERS to Classic FM may recall the feature "Something That Made Me Feel Good Today" — a brief report on what had brightened the presenter's day.

It prompted me to ask what gave a boost to people I know. At the top of her list, our friend Maisie put a warm bath and her first cup of tea, while her sister declared that nothing could beat the feel of crisp, clean sheets.

The American writer Emerson stated: "Sky is the daily bread of the eyes", while Terry Waite, who spent 1,763 days as a hostage, much of it in solitary confinement, wrote in his memoirs: "If I ever leave this place, I hope I will never forget how much pleasure very simple things gave me."

Perhaps Lakeland lover Alfred Wainwright put it in a nutshell when he wrote: "You do not need money in your pocket to walk through a field of wild flowers or on a heather moor — we have more blessings than we could ever count."

A GOLDEN MOMENT

THE FRIENDSHIP BOOK

TUESDAY—MARCH 20.

A SENIOR clerk was retiring and was being presented with a set of golf clubs. His boss said, "Mr Smith is a man who doesn't know the meaning of idleness, he doesn't know the meaning of unpunctuality or wastefulness."

"I told you," said a voice from the gathering. "We should have given him a dictionary!"

WEDNESDAY—MARCH 21.

IN 1940, the Scottish pilot of a Spitfire was fighting German aircraft over France, and was about to fire at an already-stricken Messerschmidt, when he noticed a pair of white baby's bootees hanging in the plane's cockpit.

Realising, in that split second, that the German pilot was a father like himself, the Scot lifted his finger from the firing button, and as the German lifted his left hand in grateful acknowledgement, the Scot noticed that his opponent was missing his third finger.

Years later, during the 1950s, the Scottish pilot, his wife and children were having a holiday in Bavaria, when they met a friendly family from Bremen. They spoke of their wartime experiences, and the German father said he owed his life to a Spitfire pilot — at first, not realising that he was talking to the man in question. The Scot looked down and saw the missing third finger.

The two families became firm friends — and in 1980 the German's granddaughter was married to the Scot's grandson.

THURSDAY—MARCH 22.

"WE'VE just been Spring cleaning," I said to Miriam, who was sitting next to me at the luncheon club, "and I've only just realised what hoarders we are."

Miriam laughed. "Oh, I'm a hoarder, too!" she admitted. "Always have been."

I was speechless as I reflected that Miriam lived in a small sheltered flat. How could she be a hoarder? There were very few cupboards, no attic, no cellar.

"You're wondering where I put it all, aren't you?" she asked. I nodded.

"In here," she replied, tapping her head. "Memories of loved ones, friendships, the beauty of a sunset, the golden glow of daffodils in Spring, birds singing at dawn, sunshine on rippling water . . . you just wouldn't believe what I have hoarded in my mind, ready to be recalled to help me through some rainy patches and just to enjoy, too."

Now, that's the kind of hoarding which is really worthwhile!

FRIDAY—MARCH 23.

WHILE browsing in a second-hand bookshop, I picked up an old book of prayers. Some of the prayers were in grand and lofty words, beautifully composed. The words that prompted me to buy the book, however, were written in pencil at the front:

"There is nothing that causes us to love a person so much as praying for them."

SATURDAY—MARCH 24.

IT seems appropriate that the broom bush was chosen as the emblem of the victims of suffering in Ireland during the many years of trouble there for, like the wild rose, the broom is a sign of hope. In the darkest days of Winter, broom is but a mass of thorns but once Spring comes amidst those thorns flowers suddenly blossom, filling the air with their scent.

The broom is like the crown of thorns, so once full of sorrow and suffering, yet after the crucifixion came the resurrection and with it hope for all mankind.

SUNDAY—MARCH 25.

BUT Jesus called them unto him, and said, Suffer little children to come unto me, and forbid them not: for of such is the Kingdom of God.

Luke 18:16

MONDAY—MARCH 26.

THE Lady of the House and I caught sight of a small boy crawling up a steep flight of steps one afternoon. Every so often he stopped to look back to make sure his mother was close behind him. It then occurred to me that we do much the same thing as adults.

When life becomes an uphill struggle we look for support and are encouraged when we find a friend nearby, ready to help us if we take a tumble.

TUESDAY—MARCH 27.

A FEW years after proudly graduating from an Oxford college with a science degree, a young man returned to his alma mater. This time, however, he was a don, a lecturer.

It felt very strange going back and teaching alongside some of his former lecturers. Spending time in the senior common room was something which he at first dreaded. For several days he was careful, trying to say clever things and making, he hoped, appropriate remarks whatever the topic under discussion. One day a senior lecturer walked across to him.

"My friend," he said, "I hope that you won't be offended if I give you a little piece of advice. Please don't try so hard to be clever. You see, being clever here doesn't really matter. Here we're all clever in our different ways."

"Then what does matter?"

"People will value you and remember you if you do two things – work hard and above all else be kind. That is what matters most," was the reply.

Good advice for all of us, wherever we are.

WEDNESDAY—MARCH 28.

Y OUNG David and his family were about to move house, and he was helping his mother to clear out the attic when he discovered the old family Bible. He gingerly opened it, and a dried leaf fell out of the early pages of Genesis.

"Ooh, look, Mummy!" he called out. "Adam left his clothes behind!"

GENTLE GIANTS

THURSDAY—MARCH 29.

A FRIEND has sent me what he calls his "Watch Out Collection" and I think you'll enjoy sharing these words today:

Watch your thoughts, they become words.
Watch your words, they become actions.
Watch your actions, they become habits.
Watch your habits, they become character.
Watch your character, it becomes your destiny.

FRIDAY—MARCH 30.

"THE game is never lost till won." I thought I would share George Crabbe's memorable words with you today.

Now, at first sight do you find them just a little puzzling? Well, think about them for a moment, and I am sure you will agree that they make a positive thought for today and all our tomorrows.

Born in 1754 in Aldeburgh on the coast of Suffolk, where his father was the schoolmaster and parish clerk, George was in turn country surgeon, clergyman and poet, and he wrote realistically of country people and country life.

SATURDAY—MARCH 31.

THERE used to be a popular expression, "I'll do it by and by," meaning sometime.

Our neighbour Eric used it occasionally until a friend chided him gently one day, "The Road of By and By leads to the Town of Never."

He has never said it again!

April

SUNDAY—APRIL 1.

FOR we are his workmanship, created in Christ Jesus unto good works, which God hath before ordained that we should walk in them.

Ephesians 2:10

MONDAY—APRIL 2.

HAVE you ever walked beside a river and seen children playing on stepping stones? The Lady of the House and I were out rambling one beautiful, warm day and we sat down on the grass to watch. The river was quite low and they were only in danger of getting wet feet. As we enjoyed the sunshine and listened to their laughter, I thought how life itself is a bit like stepping stones in a river.

We move from one problem and its solution to another. Sometimes the water rushes by, and we don't know how to reach the other bank. But now and then, the river is calm and we step across quite easily. Perhaps the secret is never to be afraid — step out with confidence and make the most of every stone along the way.

May your river always flow smoothly and may there always be stepping stones to help you on your way!

TUESDAY—APRIL 3.

HERE is a Spring thought for you from the pen of the poet Letitia Elizabeth Landon.

Violets! — deep blue violets!
April's loveliest coronets.

Letitia was born in the days of Jane Austen. Remembered both as a poet and a charming lady, she died young in 1838 at Cape Coast Castle, where her husband, whom she had married not long before, was Governor.

Sweet violets do not only come in blue but in deep purple, pale lavender, yellow, and lavender with a white eye. We are very fond of our little purple violet, which flowers at the bottom of the garden, a colourful reminder that Spring has arrived.

WEDNESDAY—APRIL 4.

I WAS once at a baptism, a happy occasion heightened by the minister's sense of humour.

"Ah, I see we have remembered to put some water in the basin this morning," he remarked at the start of the service. He then told us a tale of a vicar who was conducting a baptism only to find that someone had completely forgotten to fill the font with water.

With great presence of mind he asked the congregation to stand, "for the ceremony of bringing in the water," thus giving the verger an opportunity to put things right. It's nice to know that clerics can be open about making mistakes and can teach us how to be resourceful.

THE FRIENDSHIP BOOK

E NOUGH it is to be alive
*   And breathe the incense of the Spring;*
To stride along a mountain track
*   And hear exalted skylarks sing.*

Enough it is to shout like mad
*   Until the echoes tear the sky,*
Then lie upon the well-sprung turf
*   And watch the remnant clouds float by.*

Enough it is to flick the fronds
*   Of ferns which waver in the sun;*
To sit by some cascading brook
*   And dip my toes in — just for fun!*

                    Glynfab John.

FRIDAY—APRIL 6.

A MAN who stopped to read a notice was impressed by these words: "Senseless acts of beauty." Not long afterwards, he went out and planted several dozen daffodils by the roadside. This idea ties in with an article which I was reading, suggesting there is a "conspiracy of kindness" at work in the world. What a nice thought!

You can't commit a "random act of kindness" without feeling your own troubles lightened a little, while a "random act of beauty" helps to make the world around us a more attractive place. The word conspiracy sometimes has slightly sinister overtones, but a "conspiracy of kindness" is always most welcome.

SATURDAY—APRIL 7.

SOMEBODY once said that we all start off with the same size of heart, but some grow bigger than others. Edward Bulwer-Lytton wrote:

"A good heart is better than all the heads in the world," while another writer said, "There is no one alive who doesn't have a heart, but too many forget how to use it."

Go on — have a heart!

SUNDAY—APRIL 8.

THE Lord lift up his countenance upon thee, and give thee peace.

Numbers 6: 26

MONDAY—APRIL 9.

WHAT would we do without the weather as a topic of conversation? It is not only a talking point, but also affects the whole of our lives. So when I heard that a well-known weather expert was lecturing locally, I decided to go along.

I was so glad I did, because among the entertaining and informative facts he gave us was one which has stayed firmly in mind to this day — it concerns that amazing and beautiful phenomenon, the rainbow. Wherever we are standing at the moment we first catch sight of a rainbow, it may appear to be in the far, far distance, yet is actually never more than a mile to a mile and a half away.

Now, what a comforting and encouraging thought — a rainbow is nearer than we think!

THE FRIENDSHIP BOOK

TUESDAY—APRIL 10.

I PARTICULARLY admire two great men in the history of medicine. One is Edward Jenner, the other William Withering. Both worked with humble country folk, and they took notice of what their patients told them.

Jenner listened with interest to a young milkmaid's story when she told him she could not contract smallpox, because she had already had cowpox from milking the cows. Jenner realised that she had a form of immunity, and so the idea of a life-saving vaccine was born.

William Withering listened to an old country woman, who told him that by drinking a concoction of foxgloves her "dropsy" had been cured. This story enabled him to discover the properties of the plant and to isolate the drug "digitalis", which remains one of the most important heart stimulants today.

If these learned men had not listened to ordinary folk, what a great loss to medicine. We should always listen closely to what others have to say, whatever the context.

WEDNESDAY—APRIL 11.

WINIFRED HOLTBY, the author of "South Riding" and other novels made this comment: "I am quite unable to harbour resentment for long because I always forget the reason why I was originally angry."

Perhaps we should all have "poor" memories like Winifred.

SPRINGTIME
PROMISE

THE FRIENDSHIP BOOK

THURSDAY—APRIL 12.

WHEN an art group was asked to paint a picture to describe "peace", most of the students chose landscapes — placid scenes of country meadows, gentle streams and quiet woods. One girl, however, had drawn a very different picture of a city street crowded with people and traffic. In the corner was a city square and on the topmost branch of a tree a bird was singing its heart out with joy, entirely at one with the world.

She had captured the essence of real peace, an oasis of calm in an often busy and troubled world. In whatever situation you may find yourself today, I wish you the blessing of true peace.

FRIDAY—APRIL 13.

I WONDER if you have any Crown Imperials growing in your garden. They are a striking flower with large bell-shaped blooms growing on stems three feet tall. Unlike the majority of flowers, these blooms hang downwards.

The story goes that they were growing on Calvary on the day of the Crucifixion. As Christ hung on the Cross, he asked them to bow their heads in sympathy with him — but they refused.

Afterwards, when they realised what they had done, they hung their heads in shame, and their petals — which had previously been pale — turned red and purple with embarrassment. If you look carefully inside, you can see the tears they are said to have shed.

SATURDAY—APRIL 14.

HAVE you read John Masefield's play "The Trial Of Jesus"? It ends with a conversation between the Roman centurion Longinus and Pilate's wife Procula.

Longinus: He was a fine young man, my lady. Not past the middle age. And he was all alone and defied all the Jews and all the Romans.

Procula: Do you think he is dead?

Longinus: No, lady, I don't.

Procula: Then where is he?

Longinus: Let loose in the world, lady, where neither Roman nor Jew can stop his truth.

It's the message of hope that all Christian folk will be celebrating this — and every — Eastertide. A very happy Easter to you all!

SUNDAY—APRIL 15.

I CAME forth from the Father, and am come into the world: again, I leave the world, and go to the Father.
                                                          John 16:28

MONDAY—APRIL 16.

I HAD never seen Edith so chirpy. "Look," she said, pointing to a row of colourful postcards on her sideboard. I was surprised. Edith has few relatives left and only one or two close friends.

"They are from my postman!" she exclaimed. "He noticed I never get much mail so when he was on holiday he sent me one every day."

Wasn't that a lovely idea?

TUESDAY—APRIL 17.

I RATHER like this quiet and gentle modern Greek proverb, and I am sure that you will, too: "The gardens of kindness never fade".

It makes the best of thoughts for today, while Seneca the Roman philosopher reminds us: "Wherever there is a human being there is a chance for a kindness"

WEDNESDAY—APRIL 18.

I KNOW that some readers of this book belong to the older generation. I also know that they do not dwell on the topic of age. Let us remember the words of Maurice Chevalier who, at the age of 74, remarked, "I prefer old age to the alternative."

Another person once expressed the thought in a more down-to-earth way. "It's no good stopping doing things because you're getting old. It's when you stop doing things you get old."

A good recipe for long life and happiness, surely.

THURSDAY—APRIL 19.

IT'S never wise to analyse
The future with a kind
Of gloomy trait to calculate
The troubles we may find.
Whatever may occur each day
In life's demanding school,
The future's fine, if we outline —
Let Optimism Rule.
                    J. M. Robertson.

FRIDAY—APRIL 20.

DO you ever feel, I wonder, how a moment in time can be a very special one for you — and your family and friends? The Lady of the House and I were once enjoying a quiet evening at the fireside, talking about this very subject.

I was reminded of what my grandmother used to say. "Treasure every moment you have," she advised. "And treasure it all the more because you are sharing it with someone special, someone special enough to spend your time with."

SATURDAY—APRIL 21.

UNCLE BOB was teased by our family for his frequent quoting of wise sayings. Such well-known gems as, "Waste not, want not" and "A stitch in time saves nine" were uttered on appropriate occasions.

He didn't mind the teasing and always joined in the laughter. But here is one of his more original sayings, one that has stayed in mind to this day: "Sympathy is never wasted except when you give too much of it to yourself."

Uncle Bob suffered badly from arthritis but never once did I hear him complain, or expect sympathy.

SUNDAY—APRIL 22.

THE Lord is my light and my salvation; whom shall I fear? The Lord is the strength of my life; of whom shall I be afraid?

Psalms 27: 1

IN A FLAP

MONDAY—APRIL 23.

ANDREW was a little apprehensive. He was having a delicate eye operation for which he needed a local anaesthetic.

"Hold my hand," said the nurse. "If you want to tell me something, squeeze my hand."

A hand to hold, giving reassurance, comfort and a channel of communication. A healing hand, a helping hand, a guiding hand, a welcoming hand . . . Isn't it wonderful what hands can do? Whatever would we do without them?

By the way, Andrew's operation was entirely successful.

TUESDAY—APRIL 24.

IS there a new paid job or perhaps a voluntary post waiting for you? A new hobby or perhaps a task you find a little daunting? The best advice I can offer you are these words from St Augustine:

"Work as if everything depended on you, and pray as if everything depended on God!"

In this ever-changing world, it's so refreshing to come across a sentiment, unchanged for centuries, which is still as inspiring.

WEDNESDAY—APRIL 25.

I HAVE a friend who keeps these wise words on his desk:

It's nice to be important
But more important to be nice!

How true; something to keep in mind today, and every day.

THE FRIENDSHIP BOOK

TALL STORY

*A*S a friendly giraffe
  It's far better by half
To take the most distant view,
  Since with head in the clouds
Looking down on the crowds,
  I can see eye to eye with you!
Though it's often heard said
  By those widely read,
That travel soon broadens the mind —
  I'll stretch my neck out,
Just peer all about
  And horizons in plenty, I'll find.
Though the high ups may seem,
  To be proud in the extreme,
But here in defence, I must say,
  I'm never aloof,
And the ultimate proof? –
  I'll bow down to you, any day!

Elizabeth Gozney.

FRIDAY—APRIL 27.

I VERY much like these "Beauty Tips," passed on by our friend Sadie:

For attractive lips, speak words of kindness;
For lovely eyes, seek out the good in people;
For a slim figure, share your food with
  the hungry;
For poise, walk with the knowledge you'll
  never walk alone.

COUNTRY CALM

SATURDAY—APRIL 28.

THE Lady of the House returned from the hairdresser's with a beaming smile on her face. She remarked how quickly the time had flown by.

The hairdresser's three-year-old daughter had been in the salon "helping". This was unusual, but there had been a hitch with her babysitter.

"She's a lovely little girl, Francis," said the Lady of the House. "While I was waiting, we played a game with the hair rollers." I raised my eyebrows and asked what they'd done.

"Well, we made a 'tower' which didn't stand for long! Then we tried to make a 'rainbow', even though the colours were wrong, and altogether we had a lovely time." With that she went off to put the kettle on, quietly singing to herself.

The simple things in life can give the greatest pleasure. Children don't need a lot of expensive toys — only time, attention and a lot of imagination.

SUNDAY—APRIL 29.

AND Jesus said unto them, Come ye after me, and I will make you to become fishers of men.

Mark 1:17

MONDAY—APRIL 30.

A WISE man once observed that we should never undermine our worth by comparing ourselves with others; it is because we are different that each of us is special, he pointed out.

May

HAVE you ever seen a statue or carving of a young man, bald except for a long lock of hair on his forehead? It represents Kairos, the moment of opportunity. As he approaches, the story goes that you can grab him by the lock of hair, but once he has passed, nothing can drag him back.

Moments of opportunity are often only fleeting and need to be seized before they slip away for ever. Stephen Grellet wrote: "I expect to pass through this world but once; any good thing therefore that I can do, or any kindness that I can show to any fellow-creature, let me do it now; let me not defer or neglect it, for I shall not pass this way again."

If ever you are tempted to let an opportunity to do someone a good turn go by, think about Stephen Grellet — and be encouraged to try a little bit harder!

HAPPINESS is finding beauty in simple things. Delight in friendship, uplift in music, pleasure in giving — and endless joy in sharing.

STOP, LOOK AND LISTEN

THURSDAY—MAY 3.

I PARTICULARLY like this prayer in verse and hope you will, too:

I said a prayer for you today, and know God
must have heard,
I felt the answer in my heart although He spoke
no word.
I didn't ask for wealth or fame (I knew you
wouldn't mind),
I asked Him to send treasures of a far more
lasting kind.
I asked that He'd be near you at the start of
each new day,
To grant you health and blessings and friends
to share your way.
I asked for happiness for you in all things great
and small,
But it was His loving care I prayed for most
of all.

FRIDAY—MAY 4.

THE way we look at friendship can vary a lot, as I realised when I was chatting about life one afternoon with John, a neighbour. Here are some of his wise words to keep in mind:

"Just because two people argue sometimes, it doesn't mean that they don't love each other. And just because they don't argue, it doesn't always mean they do."

Sometimes spending a few minutes with a neighbour is the most worthwhile thing we'll do that day.

THE FRIENDSHIP BOOK

SATURDAY—MAY 5.

ATOP the Chiltern Hills lies the little village of Swyncombe, which boasts an 11th-century Norman church dedicated to St Botolph, an early English monk.

One of my friends called in to see this beautiful little church, and as he leafed through the visitors' book, he found this entry:

Some of you pilgrims whose journeys are long
May only visit here once, then are gone.
But four times a year I can visit this treasure.
As if that's not enough, I get paid for
   the pleasure.

The message was signed, simply — "Mick the meter-reader".

SUNDAY—MAY 6.

THE Lord shall reign for ever and ever.

Exodus 15:18

MONDAY—MAY 7.

AMERICAN philosophy always gives me a great deal to think about and this quotation is no exception. I'd like to share it with you today:

"Walking, I am listening to a deeper way. Suddenly all my ancestors are behind me. Be still, they say. Watch and listen. You are the result of the love of thousands."

In the bustle of everyday life, to pause and be still is a wonderful thing. To sense the love and the strength from the past should give us courage to face the future.

THE FRIENDSHIP BOOK

IT is sometimes observed that history books are written by the winners, and that records of what really happened are often distorted to suit whoever happens to be the victor. But I think that there are many kinds of victory, and I much prefer this view, written by the 19th-century clergyman, John Chandler:

Conquering kings their titles take
From the foes they captive make:
Jesu, by a nobler deed,
From the thousands He hath freed.

I WONDER if you've ever noticed how there are still many heroes and heroines all around us? I'm thinking more of ordinary people whose small acts of quiet courage go either unnoticed or are taken for granted.

People who disregard their own problems in order to inspire others; parents who hide their feelings of loss to encourage their offspring to gain independence; neighbours who overcome shyness to welcome a newcomer into their midst; those who brave a fear of hospitals in order to visit a lonely patient. They may not make headlines, but they are all, in their way, heroes.

In fact, there are so many different ways of showing courage that the list never ends. But perhaps one of the oddest was noted by the author Jonathan Swift: "He was a bold man that first ate an oyster."

THURSDAY—MAY 10.

HERE are a couple of sayings to savour today, from the pen of Sir James Matthew Barrie, the writer and dramatist who gave the world the enchanting story of Peter Pan:

"I am not young enough to know everything."

"We are all of us failures — at least, the best of us are."

FRIDAY—MAY 11.

AN elderly neighbour, who hates the wind and rain, asked us one Tuesday if we could do an errand for her that Thursday. We agreed, but probably looked a little surprised.

It was a beautiful morning, but Janet said quite seriously, "It's going to be a bad day on Thursday." We decided that she must have more faith in the weather forecast than we have!

Wednesday was lovely, sunny and warm, and Thursday dawned the same. We did the errand, then went for a walk in the sunshine. As we strolled through the park the Lady of the House reminded me of Janet's words, "Going to be a bad day on Thursday!"

Later when we returned, we realised how sad it was, and how she had missed a glorious day. By late evening the rain finally came, but we were by then safely tucked up in bed. As I listened to the droplets pattering on the window, I prayed: "Dear Lord, help me to keep my optimism. Let me never miss the sunshine, while waiting for the rain. Amen."

AFTER THE RAIN

SATURDAY—MAY 12.

THE first time my climbing friend Angus saw a mountain he wanted to climb it. Eventually he did just that! And the feeling of conquest on reaching the top was exhilarating, he told me.

Of course Angus couldn't stay on the hill-top — he had to return to the valley below. Isn't that just like life; we can't be on top of the world all the time. Yet when days come when the valley seems a bit too flat and hemmed in with troubles, Angus recalls the challenge of the mountain and how he conquered it. It helps him to face whatever the day may bring.

SUNDAY—MAY 13.

BEHOLD, I stand at the door, and knock: if any man hear my voice, and open the door, I will come in to him, and will sup with him and he with me.

Revelation 3: 20

MONDAY—MAY 14.

SOMEONE once said that the peoples of the world are divided into two: those who have more dinners than appetite and those who have more appetite than dinners. It's another way of saying what Robert Burns observed, "The world's ill-pairted".

Fortunately, those of us lucky enough to have more than we need can share our good fortune with others. Christian Aid Week gives us that chance.

THE FRIENDSHIP BOOK

<u>TUESDAY—MAY 15.</u>

I MUST tell you about a guest-house the Lady of the House and I once stayed in. It was full, obviously a popular place, and we were somewhat apprehensive as we realised that we'd have to share our table with another couple. Next day, we sat down, smiled and said good-morning. The couple introduced themselves as Tim and Norma.

"Now, let's see what this says today," said Norma, picking up her napkin. She read aloud from the printed corner: " 'Speak kind words and you will hear kind echoes'."

Tim read his thought for the day: " 'It's easy to be an angel when nobody's ruffling your feathers'!"

By this time there was a general buzz of conversation in the room, so I hastened to open my napkin: " 'A merry heart doeth good like a medicine'," I read aloud. From that moment all reserve disappeared — in no time we were chatting away, discussing the sayings on the napkins and laughing as if we'd known each other for years.

<u>WEDNESDAY—MAY 16.</u>

HERE are more thoughts from my notebook for you to share:

"Friendship is like seed in the garden — you cannot hurry its growth."

"It's good to have a friend you can trust, and even better to have a friend who trusts you."

"The reward of a thing well done is to have done it."

THURSDAY—MAY 17.

I WAS speaking to a student called Alice who is making a study of the Picts, the people who inhabited much of Scotland long ago. I asked her if she did not find it a rather dry subject.

"Not at all," she said. "You see, they left behind hundreds of large stones with the most beautiful carvings on them. When I study these I feel very close to the Picts."

She told me that these early artists used the same symbols and objects over and over again in their work. "Some of the symbols we don't understand," she said, "but there are also birds, fish, bulls and other animals."

What delights Alice most, though, is the mirror and comb which appear on some stones. "Though they lived such a long time ago, the Picts were not all that different. They combed their hair every morning just like I do!"

Alice has the right idea. The best way to understand people is to look, not for the differences that divide us, but for the little things which draw us all together.

FRIDAY—MAY 18.

ONE day, I'd just stamped an envelope ready for posting later when I was reminded of these words:

"Man is like a postage stamp — he gets licked, depressed, stuck in the corner, sent from pillar to post . . . but he gets there in the end, if he sticks to it."

SATURDAY—MAY 19.

DO you take your world for granted? Well, there's nothing like being with children for helping us to see the world with new eyes. Our friend Beth wrote this little verse after just such an experience.

I thought my garden dull, until my grandson
  came to stay,
And taught me how to see it in a very
    different way.
For what had once been just a lawn, now
  suddenly became
A running track where he could race, and win
  Olympic fame.
The shrubbery transformed itself to leafy
  jungle glade,
Where elephants and tigers roamed, and furry
  monkeys played.
The potting shed became a splendid spaceship
  to the stars;
The concrete gnome was suddenly a little man
  from Mars!
So many things my grandson saw, it's evidently
  plain
My garden never more will seem a boring place
  again.

SUNDAY—MAY 20.

FATHER, glorify thy name. Then came there a voice from heaven, saying, I have both glorified it, and will glorify it again.   John 12:28

GOD'S PROMISE

HE promised me He never would leave us,
Never, no never alone,
He taught us to love one another
And harvest the kindness we've sown.
He showed us the strength of the spirit
And all that our faith can achieve,
He promised the comfort of healing,
If only we trust and believe.
He told us of life everlasting,
For us, and for those we have known,
He promised He never would leave us,
Never, no never alone.

Iris Hesselden.

WHEN out on a country walk, I often catch sight of wild flowers and it is only when you get close to them that you discover how delicate they are. For many of those blooms it is a miracle that they have survived, not planted by the hand of man, but by nature — seeds blown in the wind or deposited by birds which take root to become established and bloom each year.

Those little splashes of colour make a country walk so rewarding and I am often reminded of the words spoken by Christ in Luke, chapter 12:

"Consider the lilies how they grow: they toil not, they spin not; and yet I say unto you, that Solomon in all his glory was not arrayed like one of these."

THE FRIENDSHIP BOOK

WEDNESDAY—MAY 23.

IT is not known who wrote the following lines, or when, but I feel they were probably written a long time ago. The sentiments expressed are not unusual, but doesn't the writer, he or she, express them well? I will remember these words, and I am sure you will, too, for they come from the heart:

If you have a friend worth loving,
  Love him. Yes, and let him know
That you love him, ere life's evening
  Tinge his brow with sunset glow.
Why should good words ne'er be said of
  a friend — till he is dead?
                              Anon.

THURSDAY—MAY 24

THIS "Creed" was said to have been written in New Zealand by a keen walker called A. H. Reed:
  "I believe in the gospel of work, of laughter, of goodwill to men;
  In the power of choice between good and evil, of reaping what we sow;
  In life beyond, and the imperishability of character and thought;
  In the evolution of soul;
  In God, the all-good, all-wise and ever present;
  And in Jesus Christ who revealed him to us.
  With supreme confidence I believe in the reunion of loving hearts in the hereafter."
  A fine creed to live by, surely.

FRIDAY—MAY 25.

RALPH, a wealthy businessman, always gives generously to help others. He once said to me, "Well, Francis, it's just like in my office where I have an 'in tray' and an 'out tray' for mail. A lot of good fortune comes my way. I don't let it sit in my 'in tray' — I put it in an 'out tray' and hope that it does somebody some good."

I know for a fact it does!

SATURDAY—MAY 26.

I WONDER if, when you have a friend staying with you, your goodnight farewell is "Sleep tight"? It is an expression I've often used without knowing how it originated, but on a tour round an old country house it was explained to me.

In days gone by a small truckle bed was kept underneath the large bed in the daytime and was pulled out at night so that the children could sleep on it. The base consisted of a framework of rope which became slackened during the night's sleep. If the ropes were not tightened before the following night, it resulted in an uncomfortable bed and a poor night's sleep. However, when the ropes had been made tight again, the children could "sleep tight" and enjoy a good night's rest.

With today's well-sprung mattresses, the saying no longer applies, yet it is a pleasant wish to offer our guests. I am sure we each have our own particular way of making them feel comfortable so that when we hope that they will "sleep tight", that is exactly what they will do.

SUNDAY—MAY 27.

AND Jesus, when he came out, saw much people, and was moved with compassion toward them, because they were as sheep not having a shepherd: and he began to teach them many things.

Mark 6:34

MONDAY—MAY 28.

THERE are three little words
So often hard to say —
If only we had the courage
It would be mere child's play.
Yes, it's hard to show our feelings
It seems so absurd,
And yet it is so simple
With these three little words.
They could mend many a friendship
And many a small tiff, too,
So what are those words?
Just "I love you."

Thomas Brown.

TUESDAY—MAY 29.

NOEL COWARD was the sort of witty commentator on life who always had wise words to say about this and that. Writing in his diary, he said:

"How foolish it is to think that one can ever slam the door in the face of Age. Much wiser to be polite and gracious, and ask him to lunch instead."

THE FRIENDSHIP BOOK

WEDNESDAY—MAY 30.

I READ this saying not long ago: "If we are too busy for others, we are *too* busy". I pondered on its meaning, for like so many of these adages, you really need to stop and think. Suddenly, I recalled something which happened a few years ago.

A friend's niece was visiting for a short break while studying hard for her university finals. Paula was understandably nervous and restless. "Let's go and play a game of tennis," she suggested.

But I was busy writing some letters and that seemed more important. I refused politely, then sat down at my desk. Was it conscience? I don't know, but the words just wouldn't flow, and it wasn't long before I found myself on the tennis court with Paula, enjoying a game

All too soon she was back at college, her finals were over, and she was beginning her first job. How nearly I came to missing those precious moments of shared happiness and companionship, through being "too busy".

THURSDAY—MAY 31.

HERE'S a little puzzle for you. Read this sentence: Too many people today ask, "What's in it for me?"

Now transpose the order of two two-letter words to find the answer. Got it? Yes, it now reads: "What's in *me* for *it* ?

If more people could solve this small puzzle what a different world it would be, wouldn't it?

June

FRIDAY—JUNE 1.

HERE is a delightfully fragrant thought for us all to bear in mind today:

"Happiness is a perfume inside you — when you sprinkle it on others you spill some on yourself."

SATURDAY—JUNE 2.

I OFTEN think of Hamish, a hill shepherd at Amulree in Scotland. He knew every inch of the hills which he walked in all weathers keeping an eye on his flock.

One day on holiday when I met Hamish by the roadside, I asked him if he ever felt lonely. "Never," was his firm reply. "Sheep are like people to me — they know me and I know them. When they see me on the hill they come to meet me, and there are some I've known for years, just like old friends."

When I'm out walking among the glories of nature in the countryside I often think of Hamish and these well-loved lines come to mind:

Loving Father of Thy sheep,
Keep me Lord in safety keep.
Nothing can Thy power withstand
None can pluck me from Thy hand.

THE FRIENDSHIP BOOK

SUNDAY—JUNE 3.

NOW unto God and our Father be glory for ever and ever. Amen.
Philippians 4:20

MONDAY—JUNE 4.

I WAS admiring a beautiful flower arrangement which the Lady of the House had created. "What's the secret?" I asked,

"Well," she smiled, "flowers come in all shapes and sizes and some attract more attention than others. I try to show the best in all of them. I think every flower deserves to be noticed and admired, no matter how small and humble."

Isn't it the same with people?

TUESDAY—JUNE 5.

ONE Summer's day, friends of ours travelled on *The Interceptor*, a ferry moored in London which sailed up and down the Thames. Passengers were told of the Christian significance of many of the old buildings near the river.

One very interesting aspect of the trip was that at the end of every journey there was a short time of prayer back again at Westminster — not only for new friendships made during the day, but for tourists of all nationalities who flock to see the buildings at Westminster, and the great river Thames, not forgetting their friends many miles away. Later, this little boat was moored for another night before being prepared for her new pilgrimage the following day.

WEDNESDAY—JUNE 6.

DO you know about the woman who made all the difference to life in 19th-century prisons? She was called Elizabeth Fry.

She shocked her friends and society by not only visiting people in the overcrowded and dirty prisons of the time, but also by finding clean straw and buying materials for the prisoners, so that they could make and repair their own clothes. She changed their lives, if only a little. Eventually, she persuaded friends to help her, and conditions gradually changed for the better.

Elizabeth was untiring in her efforts, setting an example which is still remembered today. We can't all be like Elizabeth Fry, but we can be aware of the needs of those around us.

An encouraging word and practical help can mean a great deal.

THURSDAY—JUNE 7.

IT was good to share in the morning assembly at our local school one Friday. I was pleased to hear the children singing with such enjoyment: "Glad that I live am I, that the sky is blue." I remember it well and it always seemed to help us start the day in the right frame of mind.

This put me in mind of Christopher Lloyd, the gardener and writer. He wrote: "The great thing in life is to fling yourself into wholehearted enjoyment of the present whenever there's something to be enjoyed."

I'll second that!

FRIDAY—JUNE 8.

*L IFE is an opportunity — benefit from it,
Life is beauty — admire it,
Life is bliss — taste it.
Life is a dream — realise it,
Life is a challenge — meet it,
Life is a duty — complete it.
Life is a game — play it,
Life is costly — care for it,
Life is wealth — keep it.
Life is love — enjoy it,
Life is a mystery — know it,
Life is a promise — fulfil it.*

Mother Teresa.

SATURDAY—JUNE 9.

A BRITISH VIP was once on an official visit to Malaya. A rather pompous man, he treated his hosts as if they were his inferiors. They reacted with courtesy but one day when he was boasting of the power he held, one of his hosts said quietly, "Sir, we have a saying in this country, 'Though a tree grow ever so high, the falling leaves return to their roots'."

The visitor went away a thoughtful man.

SUNDAY—JUNE 10.

F OR with God, nothing shall be impossible.

Luke 1:37

MONDAY—JUNE 11.

YOU know, I've always admired folk who are willing to give time to stand and rattle a collection tin in aid of some good cause or other. But it wasn't until recently that I discovered the origins of the very first flag day.

It took place in Griffithstown in Wales, on 21st August 1914, and came about simply because the young twin sons of Mrs George had nothing to do. She suggested that they should take some of her red, white and blue ribbons and make them into miniature flags. The milkman chanced to call at the house and, after admiring the boys' efforts, suggested that as the Prince of Wales had just set up a national relief fund for dependants of servicemen, they might try selling their flags in aid of this cause. It was an instant success, and Mrs George received a letter of commendation from Queen Mary.

Such a simple idea, perhaps — but how effective when put into practice by willing hands and generous hearts.

TUESDAY—JUNE 12.

THE peace talks between the African chiefs had been long and heated. When it was time for a break an elder statesman rose and said, "We may not be able to see eye to eye, but we can still walk arm in arm."

As he led his bitter enemy from the room the others followed, arms linked. By the time they all returned, they were ready to make peace.

Red Deer

THE JOURNEY

LIFE is like a journey —
A journey on a train,
Through meadows filled with buttercups
And valleys dark with rain.
The driver always knows the route
But sometimes it seems strange,
We wonder if the points are wrong
Or should the signals change?

Sometimes there are tunnels
Obscuring all the view,
But when, once more, we reach the light
The world looks fresh and new.
Enjoy the landscape on the way
One ticket's all you need,
Don't miss one moment of the trip —
The train is gath'ring speed!

Iris Hesselden.

I TURNED over the top page of my calendar one morning to show a new month's image — a picture of a busy bee about to bury itself into a colourful mass of Summer flowers. Beneath the photograph were these thought-provoking words:

"The bee that gets the honey doesn't hang around the hive".

Now, isn't that a splendid motto to keep in mind, spurring us on to greater efforts at all times of the year?

THE FRIENDSHIP BOOK

<u>FRIDAY—JUNE 15.</u>

I LIKE to make a note of some of the messages seen at wayside pulpits and here are some from my latest collection:

"God's promises will never break, no matter how hard you lean on them."

"Some people talk about finding God — as if He could get lost!"

"Faith is going out into the unknown on the strength of the known."

"If God leads you in stony paths He gives you a stout pair of shoes."

<u>SATURDAY—JUNE 16.</u>

A MOTHER and daughter were having an argument and neither was able to see the other's point of view until Grandmother intervened. She showed the wisdom of her years when she told her daughter, "You know what it's like to be young and should understand what your daughter is saying, but she has never been as old as you and will not be able to appreciate your point of view so easily.

"Remember, one day she will face the same problem with her own children, so perhaps you should set her an example now for the future!"

<u>SUNDAY—JUNE 17.</u>

HOLDING forth the world of life; that I may rejoice in the day of Christ, that I have not run in vain, neither laboured in vain.

Philippians 2:16

MONDAY—JUNE 18.

WHEN I was young, there was an old bridge over a stream near our village. This bridge was made of rope and wood and was so precarious that as you walked over clutching the ropes, it swayed to and fro and would put fear into you halfway across — or even before you started out!

To cross that bridge seemed such a challenge and to lose your nerve halfway across was not the thing to do in front of your friends. For us, life was to hold many greater challenges later on and as I think of that old bridge nowadays, I realise that we had to have faith in ourselves to cross it.

Faith is something which we need to sustain us as we go through life — faith in ourselves, faith in others and, most of all, faith in God.

TUESDAY—JUNE 19.

SITTING and thinking, or even just sitting and thinking of nothing in particular, can be a soothing and relaxing occupation. Some people find it very difficult to switch off and be still, and yet this is something we all need now and then.

To watch the tide ebb and flow, the clouds drift by, or even the rain on the window can give us an inner peace, helping to recharge our batteries. For a little while we can let the noisy world go on its way. I found these lines one day: "Sitting quietly, doing nothing, Spring comes and the grass grows by itself".

What a wealth of peace and serenity in just a few words.

THE FRIENDSHIP BOOK

WEDNESDAY—JUNE 20.

A TOURIST in an English country market town asked a policeman why so many people had gathered in the town square to watch the arrival of a wedding party. Was it someone well known? Was it of special importance?

The policeman turned to the visitor and replied, "*All* weddings are important."

The subject of weddings reminds me of the answer given by Henry Ford when he was asked, on his Golden Wedding day, for the secret of a happy married life. He said, "The formula is the same that I have always used for making cars — just stick to one model."

THURSDAY—JUNE 21.

SOME neighbours near the small cottage where we once spent a holiday left us with a happy memory of our stay. An elderly couple had a lovely garden which we often passed on our walks. One day, they showed us around. Above all, we admired the variety of plants in their herb garden. They sold vegetables and flowers at the gate, so we decided to buy some before we returned home.

On opening our purchases later, the Lady of the House and I were filled with delight. On top of the bag of potatoes, carrots and green vegetables lay an attractive bunch of mixed herbs which could be planted in our own garden. Now, when we gather herbs from our garden we still feel a glow as we think of our friends' kindness which has forged a lasting bond of friendship.

FRIDAY—JUNE 22.

"I LIKE cats and dogs very much indeed," wrote Jerome K. Jerome, author of "Three Men In A Boat". "They never say unkind things. They never tell us of our faults 'merely for our own good.' . . . They are always glad to see us. They are with us in all our humours . . . And when we bury our face in our hands and wish we had never been born, they don't sit up very straight and observe that we have brought it all upon ourselves.

"But they come up softly; and shove their heads against us. If it is a dog, he looks up at you with his big true eyes and says with them, 'Well, you've always got me, you know. We'll go through the world together, and always stand by each other, won't we?'"

It's a lovely description of the devotion and fidelity of pets. I'm sure that all animal lovers will understand exactly what Jerome K. Jerome meant.

SATURDAY—JUNE 23.

I DON'T know who first spoke these words but surely they are worthy of our attention, not just today but every day:

If you can't have the best of everything,
Then make the best of everything you have.

SUNDAY—JUNE 24.

AND he said unto them, Go ye into all the world, and preach the gospel to every creature.

Mark 16: 15

THE FRIENDSHIP BOOK

MONDAY—JUNE 25.

WHEN Wimbledon fortnight comes round, like thousands of others, I'm glued to my television set. My eyes are on the tennis players and the exciting games, but in the background, doing their job efficiently and unobtrusively, ball boys and girls.

Each year there are hundreds of applicants from nearby schools and 182 are selected. Then there is training to achieve a high standard of physical fitness and discipline. They don't get paid — they do it for the honour of being at Wimbledon.

Traditionally, the two flower girls who present bouquets to the royal party are chosen from those working on the outer courts to give those not in the centre court a chance to shine.

As in tennis, we may not all have the opportunity to "play on the centre court", and perhaps we would not wish to, but let's never underestimate the importance of a supportive role and its value to others.

TUESDAY—JUNE 26.

I'M sure that we all, at some time or other, have heard or read something that a famous person has said, but we do not always hear much of what ordinary people have said. Well, I have found what someone unknown — for no credit is given to this author — said about true wisdom:

"Wisdom is the art of knowing exactly when to speak your mind and when to mind your speech."

TWO'S COMPANY

THE FRIENDSHIP BOOK

ROBERT a widower, has just retired and started a new chapter in his life. As a farewell gift, his colleagues bought him a computer, and he has spent hours in front of the screen learning how to use it. He's now very proficient with his word processing program.

"You know, Francis," he observed one day, "these computers are marvellous machines, but one of the best things about them is that you can undo your mistakes. For example, if you accidentally delete whole pages of text, you can retrieve them at the touch of a button. Wouldn't it be wonderful if we had an 'undo' facility in life? Think how many of life's mistakes you could fix, how much unhappiness could be turned to joy just at the touch of a button!"

Now, wouldn't we all love to be able to undo an earlier wrong in our lives?

OUR young friend, Fiona, could be heading for a bright literary career when she grows up. Why? Well, she loves to write short letters to her friends.

One of her recent letters was addressed this way: "To my friend, God." Then she went on — "Dear God, I didn't think orange went with purple until I saw the sunset you made on Tuesday. That was cool!" *Fiona*.

Now, there speaks someone who already has a keen appreciation of the beauties of nature.

FRIDAY—JUNE 29.

ONE of my primary school teachers had a wealth of maxims, intended to guide us along life's way. One was the warning: "Be sure your sins will find you out."

I was reminded of this when I read a story about a butcher. A customer had asked him for a chicken and when one was produced she asked, "Have you a larger one?" The butcher knew it was the only one left but he said, "I'll see," then went into his back room. There he fluffed up the bird and, walking back into the shop, flourished it and asked, "How about this one, then?"

"That's perfect!" exclaimed his customer. "I'll take both of them!" We are not told what happened next, but my teacher would doubtless have said, "It served him right," and added another maxim: "Honesty is the best policy."

SATURDAY—JUNE 30.

I HEARD this thought-provoking tale not long ago. A man looked up to heaven and asked, "God, what is a million years to you?"

"A million years to me is like a second to you," came the reply.

The man then asked, "What is a million pounds to you?"

"A million pounds to me is like a penny to you."

Then the man asked, "God, can I have a million pounds?"

"Certainly," replied God. "In a second."

July

SUNDAY JULY 1.

THEREFORE, my beloved brethren, be ye stedfast, unmoveable, always abounding in the work of the Lord, forasmuch as ye know that your labour is not in vain in the Lord.

Corinthians 1 15:58

MONDAY—JULY 2.

THERE has been a new addition to our friends Rob and Elsa's household — a delightful Siamese kitten called Mischief. However, we all wondered whether he would be accepted and indeed be safe in a home where there were already two large and boisterous dogs. We needn't have worried, though, for the animals quickly adapted to being together all the time and now they live in harmony.

It brought to mind the Walt Disney film "The Fox And The Hound" about the fox cub and the fox hound puppy who met through the garden fence and struck up a close friendship. They didn't realise they were meant to be enemies and as they grew older, they stuck together through thick and thin, always coming to the rescue if the other was in danger.

I often think that the animal world can teach us a thing or two!

TUESDAY—JULY 3.

A NEW neighbour, Jim, had spent the weekend trying to restore some order to an overgrown garden he had inherited. Noticing him struggling to load a trailer with barrow-loads of branches, old bushes and hedge clippings, I paused to help and took the opportunity to compliment him on his work.

"Why, thank you," he responded. "And I hope it will look even better by the time I've landscaped the whole garden."

I wished Jim luck with his efforts, smiling at his infectious enthusiasm. How right he had been about the satisfaction to be gained by disposing of rubbish.

Now, perhaps we should take the idea a step further, and add different kinds of debris to the list — old grudges, petty jealousies, and all those other unwanted items which sometimes clutter our lives. How glorious it would be to be rid of them for good!

WEDNESDAY—JULY 4.

*N*O *matter what prescriptions*
Are being handed out,
The best medicine is laughter,
Of that there's little doubt.
Its benefits are reckoned
To have guarantees that say —
A dose of it's essential
To be taken day by day.

J. M. Robertson.

THE FRIENDSHIP BOOK

THURSDAY— JULY 5.

I SMILED when I saw this notice pinned on the noticeboard beside the reception desk in a busy guest-house one Summer:

Guests are at liberty to brag as much as they like while they are here. Nobody will ever know how unimportant you are back home!

FRIDAY—JULY 6.

WHEN little Lucy was invited to take part in one of our Sunday School services she was very pleased. However, when the day arrived and she stood up in front of everybody, she couldn't remember the words she had so carefully learned. Fortunately, her mother was in the front pew and whispered, "I am the Light of the World."

Lucy's face brightened. "My mum is the light of the world," she began confidently. There were smiles at her innocent mistake, but understanding nods, too, as we all remembered afresh that mothers are indeed the light of the world.

SATURDAY—JULY 7.

THE Songs Of Praise team once did a series with the theme "Sacred Places" visiting many locations in the United Kingdom — cathedrals, country churches, ruined abbeys and so on.

Many of us have our own private place which brings us a special sense of inner peace. As the naturalist David Bellamy said, "All you have to do is walk this world with wonder in your heart."

Now, there's a lovely thought!

SUNDAY—JULY 8.

ALL the paths of the Lord are mercy and truth unto such as keep his covenant and his testimonies.

Psalms 25:10

MONDAY—JULY 9.

ARE you the kind of person who thrives on change, or do you dislike it? We all know, deep down, that without change there can be no progress. The greatest explorers and inventors must have relished change, welcoming it with open arms. However, for the rest of us it can sometimes be rather upsetting.

I came across these words: "Everything changes, nothing remains the same. And letting go of the way things are, anticipating instead what they might become, frees us to live each moment more fully". The quote ends with the words: "And the present has come to teach us".

Perhaps, if we can bear this in mind, we won't be quite so resentful about change. We may also learn new lessons, both from the present and from the future.

TUESDAY—JULY 10.

LESS well known than his famous poem about daffodils is William Wordsworth's memorable advice: "No endeavour is in vain, its reward is in its doing."

Words worth considering today, aren't they?

WEDNESDAY—JULY 11.

VISITING an elderly arthritic friend living in a village some miles away, I remarked how cosy she looked and how lovely her flowers were on the sideboard.

"I have Mollie to thank for them — for everything, in fact," Jane replied. Mollie is her home help, but she is more than that, a true friend and an absolute treasure, for whom nothing is ever too much trouble.

I learned that Mollie does many kindnesses to others who live in the village, too — she fetches Mrs Jackson's pension, mows Mr Jones' lawn and provides transport to the station for anyone who needs it.

"She must be a remarkable young woman," I remarked.

"Young!" exclaimed Jane. "She's not much younger than me. I said to her only the other day — Mollie, why don't you retire? You don't need to work now, surely."

"Oh, yes, I do," she retorted smartly. "What on earth would I do with my time — and what would all my friends do without me?"

There was no answer to that.

THURSDAY—JULY 12.

HERE is a thought for today — and one for every day:

"Let us not look back in anger, nor forward in fear, but around in awareness."

James Thurber.

FRIDAY—JULY 13.

HELP me to be strong, Lord,
So I can help another,
Help me to have wisdom
And so advise a friend.
Teach me to be patient
With greater understanding,
Let me be a channel
For all the love You send.
Even more than these, Lord,
Teach me to be humble,
Without You I am nothing
And cannot find the way.
Teach me how to listen,
For prayers are always answered,
Help me to be grateful
And thankful every day.

Iris Hesselden.

SATURDAY—JULY 14.

THESE lines were brought to my attention by a Canadian correspondent: "Grant me the quiet charm which friendship gives, which lives unchanged and cheers me while it lives."

John R. Newell (1881)

I thought that they would make pleasing reading for you today.

SUNDAY—JULY 15.

FOR I know that my redeemer liveth, and that he shall stand at the latter day upon the earth.

Job 19:25

MEADOWSWEET

MONDAY—JULY 16.

HAPPINESS, as defined by many writers, is always around us and nearer than we may realise. Here are some of my favourite definitions:

"The happiest person is the person who thinks the most interesting thoughts."

"From contentment with little comes happiness."

And this last one seems to hold the key:

"We are happy when, for everything inside us, there is a corresponding something outside us."

May your own "butterfly of happiness" settle gently on your shoulder.

TUESDAY—JULY 17.

WE have lived at our present home for a long time. When we first arrived, we were delighted to own a garden, although it was very neglected. We dug and weeded, weeded and dug for months. It seemed that the back-breaking work would never end.

One warm sunny morning the Lady of the House and I stood for a moment to admire our newly-beautiful garden. I was particularly busy at the time, and perhaps the Lady of the House was, too, because she suddenly said, "You know, Francis, if we tackle the tasks in life as we tackled the garden, we will one day be able to stand back like this and see the good results we have gained."

I am sure she is right. I went indoors still thinking about it, and now when life gets tough I always remember our garden miracle.

THE FRIENDSHIP BOOK

WEDNESDAY—JULY 18.

THERE'S something about a new set of shelves which is irresistible — somehow, they just have to be put to use immediately. So it was with delight that on my new shelves I set out books, sorting them into subjects, smoothing down covers and pages. As I arranged the titles, I remembered the carpenter who had done that fine job for me.

I'd noticed how meticulously he measured the wood he was using. Having measured once, he went back and checked his calculations again. "Is it right this time?" I'd asked.

"It was right the first time, as it happened," he replied, "but I was trained to follow the carpenter's golden rule — 'measure twice before you saw once'."

Now, whenever I take a book from my shelves, I recall that rule, and I'm sure it has saved me from many an unwise action or word.

THURSDAY—JULY 19.

ERIC LOMAX, a former British Army officer and author of the best-selling book "The Railway Man", worked on the notorious Burma Death Railway during the Second World War. Of all the Japanese who ill-treated him one face particularly stood out.

For years Eric longed for revenge but, in the end, when he and the man met, he forgave him. The two became friends — "blood brothers" as they put it — and the burden each carried was finally lifted.

FRIDAY—JULY 20.

HAVE you noticed how many authors dedicate their book along these lines: "To my wife — or husband — for patience, understanding and help"?

Now, not everyone is a published author, but thousands of couples each year pay sincere tributes in writing to their partners. When silver, ruby, golden or even diamond weddings come round, many fond tributes to couples are often published in the local press.

How much happiness and depth of feeling is shown in these words and we realise that each partnership will have shown a great deal of courage and fortitude in troubled times, as well as enjoying happy days together.

SATURDAY—JULY 21.

HERE are two sayings from my collection to inspire you today:

The future is waiting —
Untouched, untrodden, undiscovered.
Go ahead, be a new explorer!

"Friendship chases away dark clouds, discovers unexpected laughter, and makes this world a better place."

SUNDAY—JULY 22.

IF ye love me, keep my commandments.

John 14:15

MONDAY—JULY 23.

LOVING someone makes this world a better place. It lifts the heart like the first rose in Summer, the first snowdrop in Winter, the first blackbird in Spring.

Love gives, to each one of us, a glimpse of Heaven here on earth.

TUESDAY—JULY 24.

THE Wallington Missionary Auctions in Surrey is an auction sale with a difference. It is a registered charity for raising money towards the support of missionary societies and Christian outreach at home and overseas.

The project was begun in the late 1950s by Vernon Hedderly who had the vision that Christians could be encouraged to turn out their chosen cherished possessions to release money for missions.

Auctions are held six times a year and anything saleable is acceptable but in particular antique furniture, silver, jewellery, pictures, musical instruments, clocks, coins and medals. The valuers and auctioneers are all experts and give their services free. Donors are told how much their gift has raised and proceeds are allocated according to their wishes. In addition bric-à-brac sold on huge stalls before each auction raises considerable sums annually.

The society's motto, appropriately, is: "When you give, others live."

WEDNESDAY—JULY 25.

MANY of us are keen on recycling used materials, doing something to help preserve the environment — perhaps collecting our empty bottles and then going to our local bottle bank.

A recycling enthusiast was once strolling over a patch of grassy parkland on which many cars were parked. He happened to see a crumpled drinks can lying on the grass, a sight which upset his tidy mind, and he at once retrieved the can to add to his store of materials for recycling.

To his surprise he was soon surrounded by a group of complaining children shouting: "You've moved one of our goalposts!"

Recycling leads to re-using, so perhaps they were recycling that can in another way.

THURSDAY—JULY 26.

OPTIMISM is a quality we might define as the tendency to take the most hopeful view of all matters. That is exactly what a church meeting did one cloudy day when discussing ways to raise money for deserving causes.

"Let's start sunshine boxes," someone suggested. "Every family could put a 20 pence piece into a box each day the sun shines as a thank-you offering."

Laughter greeted this idea and some argued that too little money would be made, given our climate, but they were outvoted. And when the boxes were later emptied they were able to spread more than a "little sunshine" to those in need.

FRIDAY—JULY 27.

THE Lady of the House has quite a collection of fridge magnets in our kitchen. Imagine how pleased she was when she received a surprise addition to her collection.

A young friend of ours had returned from holiday and, with a shy smile, Mark handed her a small and rather crumpled paper bag. He insisted the gift had been paid for with his own pocket money, and his mother confirmed that this was true. However, we did feel she had helped with his choice, for these were the words:

"Warning! — The road to success is always under construction".

After they left, it was given pride of place as we considered the wisdom and truth of these words. Very rarely does success come overnight — it has to be worked for, something which our young friend will need to find out for himself!

SATURDAY—JULY 28.

HERE is a challenging saying to consider from the pen of André Maurois, the French author: "Growing old is no more than a bad habit which a busy man has no time to form."

SUNDAY—JULY 29.

JESUS said unto him, Thou shalt love the Lord thy God with all thy heart, and with all thy soul, and with all thy mind.   Matthew 22:37

PALM, POOL
AND PEACE

MONDAY—JULY 30.

IT'S a long time since I first saw this epitaph, but two centuries after the death of George Routledge, it is worth recalling the attributes assigned to this man commemorated in the churchyard at Lydford in Devon:

Here lies in a horizontal position the outside case of

GEORGE ROUTLEDGE
Watchmaker

Integrity was the mainspring and prudence the regulator of all the actions of his life — humane, generous and liberal, his hand never stopped till he had relieved distress.

So nicely regulated were his movements that he never went wrong, except when set going by people who did not know his key. Even then he was easily set right again.

He had the art of disposing of his time so well, till his hours glided away, his pulse stopped beating.

He ran down November 14th, 1801, aged 57.

In hopes of being taken in hand by his Maker, thoroughly cleaned, repaired, wound up and set going in the world to come, when time shall be no more.

TUESDAY—JULY 31.

WHEN trust is sometimes fragile
  And needs intensive care,
To strengthen, try devotion
  And treat with extra prayer.

Elizabeth Gozney.

August

WEDNESDAY—AUGUST 1.

A FRIEND collects odd notices seen around the world. Here are a few:

"We take your bags and send them in all directions".

(Seen in a Copenhagen airline ticket office).

"If this is your first visit to our country, you are welcome to it."

(Seen in a Moscow hotel room).

"Only enter the lift when lit up".

(A Leipzig elevator).

They say travel broadens the mind but it can also broaden your smile. Can you add any more to this lighthearted list after your holiday this year?

THURSDAY—AUGUST 2.

A LTHOUGH John Ruskin's later life was such a sad one as visitors to his Lakeland home, Brantwood, at Coniston, realise, he left much wisdom and knowledge for future generations. One piece of his advice is as valid today as when he first gave it:

"In every person that comes near you look for what is good and strong. Honour that, rejoice in it and as you can imitate it."

FRIDAY—AUGUST 3.

ROBERT LOUIS STEVENSON, the author of such well-loved classics as "Treasure Island" and "Kidnapped", wrote: "Though we steer after a fashion, yet we must sail according to the winds and currents."

Wise, thoughtful words to remember, when circumstances do not allow us to follow our chosen path through life but make us take another quite different one. Walk that path with good heart — you may well find it more rewarding in terms of experiences and achievements at the end of the day than you could ever have hoped!

SATURDAY—AUGUST 4.

PLANT IT NOW!

"GREAT oaks from little acorns grow"
Is what we're often told.
Those small beginnings tend to show
Such wonders to behold.
In a way it fashions hope
For people to agree
The seed of friendship given scope
Can grow tree-mendously.
J.M. Robertson.

SUNDAY—AUGUST 5.

FOR God so loved the world, that he gave his only begotten Son, that whosoever believeth in him should not perish, but have everlasting life.
John 3: 16

MONDAY—AUGUST 6.

ON a beautiful Summer's day the Lady of the House and I visited the Norfolk home of Charlotte Jane King. Charlotte's embroidered sampler dated 1792, when she was twelve years old, and sewn in once-bright crimson, blue and green threads, still hangs in her father's library.

As well as trees, flowers, birds and many other things, Charlotte neatly stitched these lines by Francis Beaumont and John Fletcher, both play-wright contemporaries of Shakespeare.

That place that does contain
My books, the best of company is to me,
A glorious Court where hourly I converse.

Friends come in many guises!

Incidentally, when Charlotte was a wife and mother, she herself wrote a succession of children's books, two of which sit on the shelves in our library at home. I think for many children, they must indeed have been "the best of company".

TUESDAY—AUGUST 7.

I LIKE this quotation from the Greek philoso-pher Plato. It is the kind of wise thought that is surely worth remembering:

"I know not how I may seem to others, but to myself I am but a small child wandering upon the vast shores of knowledge, every now and then finding a small bright pebble to content myself with."

WEDNESDAY— AUGUST 8.

I LIKE these lines by Eustace Budgell, written in 1712, and think they will also strike a chord with many readers:

"Friendship is strong and habitual in two persons to promote the good and happiness of one another."

THURSDAY—AUGUST 9.

WE had decided that we would be staying in all day as the weather was so bad. The rain had been heavy since early morning and by lunchtime we had thunder and lightning. Rather disappointing for Summer, though not unusual in our climate.

About four o'clock the clouds suddenly broke and the sun came out, so the Lady of the House and I thought we might venture out for a little stroll. The moment we stepped outdoors we felt the warm air on our faces, but even more noticeable was the scent of flowers and blossom. The rain had really refreshed the gardens and trees, and the perfume was delightful.

I thought of the beautiful music in Beethoven's Pastoral Symphony "Thanksgiving After The Storm." Later, I found myself thinking how much our lives are like the weather — sunny and rainy spells, peaceful moments and troubled times — yet we have so many blessings to be grateful for. Perhaps, now and then, we should pause and count them and have our own "thanksgiving after the storm."

FRIDAY—AUGUST 10.

SANDY STEWART was a travelling man, a well-known figure with a white beard and unruly hair, always carrying a stick as he trod the highways and byways of Scotland.

He had served King and Country in the Black Watch but after the Second World War had turned his back on society for reasons known only to himself, and took to the open road. For over 30 years Sandy was a familiar figure as he tramped the roads. He once said:

"A house I have not but the sky is my roof, the earth my floor, the hills my walls, and my windows are my eyes."

SATURDAY—AUGUST 11.

HOW many times have you laughed today? No, it's not a silly question. I ask because of something the Lady of the House once read to me from a serious analytical study of the gentle art of laughter.

Apparently, four-year-olds laugh an average of 450 times a day, and adults a mere 15 times. We would surely do well to look at this fascinating and often amusing world through the eyes of a child.

SUNDAY—AUGUST 12.

GRACE be with all them that love our Lord Jesus Christ in sincerity. Amen. Ephesians 6:24

THE FRIENDSHIP BOOK

MONDAY—AUGUST 13.

ON a visit to St Olave's Church in York, I was delighted to discover little mice carved into several of the choirstalls — the trademark of Robert "Mousey" Thompson of Kilburn. Likewise, in the Sound of Harris is the little island of Ensay, which boasts but one house and a private Episcopal church with an oak door upon which can be found the carved mouse which bears witness to its origin in Kilburn.

Robert Thompson was a craftsman of some repute, who also made furniture and whose special signature was that little carved mouse which is both an attraction to all who discover it, and also serves as a reminder that Kilburn's most famous craftsman was once as poor as a church mouse.

It was Robert Thompson's way of thanking God.

TUESDAY—AUGUST 14.

IN a church hall I came on this notice:

SIX RULES
*The six most important words: "I admit that I
  was wrong!"*
*The five most important words: "You did a
  great job."*
*The four most important words: "Consider others
  – not yourself."*
The three most important words: "May I help?"
The two most important words: "Thank you!"
The one most important word: "We."
The least important word: "I".
These words add up to a lot of good sense.

WEDNESDAY—AUGUST 15.

I SOMETIMES wonder if the word "trust" has lost some of its meaning nowadays. This story from three centuries ago has much to tell us.

In November 1692 William Penn and his fellow colonists made a Treaty of Friendship with the American Indians. The white men carried no weapons; the Indians were fully armed. Penn said:

"The Great Spirit who made me and you, who rules the heavens and the earth, and knows the innermost thoughts of men, knows that I and my friends have a hearty desire to live in peace and friendship with you, and to serve you to the uttermost of our power. It is not our custom to use hostile weapons against our fellow creatures, for which reason we have come unarmed."

I would call that getting off to a good start with your neighbours.

THURSDAY—AUGUST 16.

I N our street is a young family who recently moved there from another town. The couple have a son who is six years old, and he has been taught to say The Lord's Prayer every night.

The Lady of the House heard this story from the youngster's mother: "I was standing out of sight behind the bedroom door listening to Edward saying his prayers. He was word perfect until I heard him say, 'Give us this day our daily bread and deliver us some e-mail —'"

Such is the influence of computers in the modern world . . .

GRACIOUS GABLES

FRIDAY—AUGUST 17.

HOPE means such a lot to all of us, doesn't it? Every day there is something to hope for. It could simply be a surprise letter or a phone call, or perhaps a visit from someone we haven't seen for a while. Maybe some warm sunshine for a special day out or for pottering in the garden. For those who are not feeling well, the hope of improvement; for those facing exams or interviews, the hope of success.

Someone once said, "I live on hope and so, I think, do all who come into this world."

These words I once read are also descriptive and somehow more comforting: "In the kingdom of hope, there is no Winter."

What a lovely thought! May we all continue to live and to flourish in that beautiful place.

SATURDAY—AUGUST 18.

OUR thoughts are living things —
They travel through time and space,
They comfort us when we are lonely,
They bring us closer when we're apart,
They heal us when we are sick.
Thoughts — like love — are indestructible.
Never underestimate the power of your thoughts.

SUNDAY—AUGUST 19.

I AM Alpha and Omega, the beginning and the ending, saith the Lord, which is, and which was, and which is to come, the Almighty.

Revelation 1:8

THE FRIENDSHIP BOOK

I ATTENDED the christening of a new arrival in our family circle, a happy occasion when relatives and friends gathered to support the baby and his parents with good wishes and prayer.

There was a cake to be shared afterwards and presents, too, and many promises of practical help for the future from grandparents, godparents, aunts and uncles. It brought to mind these words:

"If a child lives with security, he learns to
  have faith.
If a child lives with fairness, he learns justice.
If a child lives with encouragement, he learns
  confidence.
If a child lives with tolerance, he learns to
  be patient.
If a child lives with acceptance and friendship,
He learns to find love in the world."

Wise words — and just as important for older folk, too.

THE following lines contain words to comfort us, when we have been proved wrong about somebody or something, and have had the courage to admit it. These words were written by Jonathan Swift, the author of that famous classic "Gulliver's Travels":

"A man should never be ashamed to own he has been in the wrong, which is but saying in other words, that he is wiser today than he was yesterday."

REFLECTED GLORY

THE FRIENDSHIP BOOK

WEDNESDAY—AUGUST 22.

HERE are some thoughts for you to consider today:

Don't lose your temper — keep it safely hidden.

Don't look back on defeat — look forward to success.

Slow progress is better than no progress.

THURSDAY—AUGUST 23.

I'D like to share with you this letter I received from my friend Derek: "Dear Francis, – Whether it was a bad dream, or I'd eaten unwisely at suppertime, I don't know, but I woke up this morning with a 'black dog' on my shoulder.

"I began by tackling various chores to take my mind off things, but the 'black dog' wouldn't budge. Later, I sat down at my desk feeling sure that the pile of letters, usually so welcome, would lift my mood. Not a bit of it. I nodded grateful thanks for the arrival of coffee and biscuits.

"Then, a fluttery shadow at the window caught my eye — it was a pigeon, closely followed by his mate. I opened the window and crumbled a biscuit on to the sill. On the inside windowsill were several plants, and I decided to water them right away.

"Then I sat down to drink my coffee, and suddenly I felt good — the 'black dog' had slunk away at last.

"Could it be to do with the few simple tasks, looking after other living things? See if it works for you next time all is not well with your world".

FRIDAY—AUGUST 24.

"THAT wasn't a very nice thing to say," said a schoolgirl reprovingly to her companion as they walked past my garden gate. I wondered if she had been taught to think before speaking as many of we older ones were, and to ask the question:

Is it true?
Is it necessary?
Is it kind?
If not, it is probably better not said.

It is still wise advice and the world would be a much better place if we took it seriously.

SATURDAY—AUGUST 25.

WHEN your road is all uphill
And twisting all about,
Just have a little courage
And never, ever doubt.
When your goal is out of sight
And hidden from your view,
Keep looking for a rainbow
And know you will win through.
When your plans have gone astray,
Your heart is not as light,
Just have a little courage
And things will turn out right.

Iris Hesselden.

SUNDAY—AUGUST 26.

BUT he that is joined unto the Lord is one spirit.

Corinthians I 6:17

THE FRIENDSHIP BOOK

DOING a spot of weeding one morning, I heard a neighbour singing as she pegged out her washing. "You sound very cheerful," I said. "Has something nice happened?"

"No!" Peggy laughed. "I was just serenading my soul." And she sang more brightly than ever, making me feel like joining in.

Then one of those coincidences happened, as they do so often in life. Not long afterwards, I was listening to a science programme and the lecturer began talking about the value of singing. He went on to say that there was a scientific reason why singing is good for us; apparently it leads to the release of endorphins, which make us feel good.

So, sing on, even if it's behind closed doors — you'll feel good! And if you feel good, so will those around you.

A FRIEND of ours keeps a note of the unusual things her grandchildren have said. Ethel's book is already well filled, and here's a tale she added to her collection not long ago.

Grandson Duncan had asked, just as grandchildren tend to do, "Grandma, what age are you?"

Teasingly, and with a friendly smile, she replied, "I'm not quite sure."

The youngster had the perfect, if surprising, solution. "Well, then, Grandma," he advised, "Why don't you look in your underwear? Mine says that I'm four!"

TWICE AS NICE

THE FRIENDSHIP BOOK

THE German poet and dramatist Johann Wolfgang von Goethe once wrote down his eight requisites for contented living. Two hundred years later, they are still worth reading:

Health enough to make work a pleasure;
Wealth enough to support your needs;
Strength to battle with difficulties and
*   overcome them;*
Grace enough to confess your sins and
*   forsake them;*
Patience enough to toil until some good
*   is accomplished;*
Charity enough to see some good in
*   your neighbour;*
Faith enough to make real the things of God;
Hope enough to remove all anxious
*   fears concerning the future.*

"HAPPINESS," said the Lady of the House, "is like perfume."

"How do you make that out?" I asked.

"Because if you sprinkle it around, you can't help spilling a few drops on yourself."

I could have added that it's also free!

ONE of my favourite teachers at school once said to us, "Remember, you can rub out the mistakes in your jotters in the classroom, but you can't rub them out in the book of life."

September

A NEW neighbour, John, came to tea one Sunday and while telling us a little about his life, told the Lady of the House and me this charming tale. He had spent some time working in the Far East and, on one occasion, had stayed with an elderly Chinese official for four days. During a shared meal, the wise old gentleman told him of his beliefs.

"Our lives are shaped, not only by our own efforts," he said, "but also by the influence of all the people we have met during our lifetime. When we reach old age, we have become a polished jewel, the product of all those that we have met over the years."

John said that after this, he thought of all those who had contributed to the polishing of his jewel, and he was thereafter influenced by his Chinese host to try to contribute positively to the lives of all those he met.

A ND this is the will of him that sent me, that every one which seeth the Son, and believeth on him, may have everlasting life: and I will raise him up at the last day.

John 6:40

THE FRIENDSHIP BOOK

MONDAY—SEPTEMBER 3.

"NEVER too busy to help." That could have been the motto of the industrious and successful 19th-century author Anthony Trollope.

Early life was difficult for him, both during his schooldays and later when working as a junior in the post office. Yet years later he became a surveyor for the post office, a position with a great deal of responsibility. His travels around England and Ireland gave him knowledge of people and places which was invaluable for his novels.

In spite of his official work and time spent writing he was never too busy to help anyone in trouble, especially less successful authors. We can follow Anthony Trollope's example by helping other people when we can, and never being too busy to help.

TUESDAY—SEPTEMBER 4.

I RECEIVED a letter from a friend who quoted these wise words to me:

Whatever our hands touch —
We leave fingerprints!
On walls, on furniture,
On doorknobs, dishes, books,
As we touch we leave our identity.

Oh, please, wherever I go today,
Help me leave heartprints!
Heartprints of compassion,
Of understanding, and love.
Heartprints of kindness and genuine concern.

WEDNESDAY—SEPTEMBER 5.

I FOUND an interesting item in a church magazine sent to me from Yorkshire. A young boy was trying to help his mother store apples. Putting his arms around too many, and trying to carry them all at once, out they dropped one by one until they were all on the floor.

Laughing, his mother put his hands round one apple. "There, take that one and carry the rest the same way," she suggested. Now grown up, that young man can say: "It taught me a useful lesson. Don't try to put your arms round a year or even a week. Say, 'Here is another day begun, Lord, help me to live it for You. Give me now the help and strength I need.' "

If we try to carry all tomorrow's burdens today we may collapse under the load. It's far better to take one step at a time: "Do not worry about tomorrow for it will worry about its own things."

THURSDAY—SEPTEMBER 6.

HERE'S a worthwhile thought for today, from the writer Arnold Glashow:

"Nothing lasts for ever — not even your troubles".

FRIDAY—SEPTEMBER 7.

A CORRESPONDENT has never forgotten her young grandson's choice description of a particularly attractive sunrise.

As it rose behind some fluffy white clouds, he said, "Look, Nanna, sunshine with cream on it!"

THE FRIENDSHIP BOOK

SATURDAY—SEPTEMBER 8.

FRIENDSHIP can't be hurried,
* So handle it with care,*
For like the rose's fragrance
* And the blossoms it will bear,*
True friendship's bonds will strengthen,
* And deepen every day,*
The kind that never falters
* Or ever fades away.*
And though the roses' season
* Must ere too soon depart,*
The season of true friendship
* Lasts forever in the heart.*
                    Elizabeth Gozney.

SUNDAY—SEPTEMBER 9.

WHILE I live will I praise the Lord: I will sing praises unto my God while I have any being.   Psalms 146:2

MONDAY—SEPTEMBER 10.

I CAME across this verse one evening. It's a reminder of all we have to be thankful for, especially at harvest time:

Bread is a lovely thing to eat, God bless the barley
* and the wheat.*
A lovely thing to breathe is air, God bless the
* sunshine everywhere.*
The earth's a lovely place to know, God bless the
* folk that come and go.*
Alive's a lovely thing to be, Giver of life, we say
* Bless Thee.*

BRANCHING OUT

TUESDAY—SEPTEMBER 11.

HAPPINESS is not as elusive as some may think, as the writer of this anonymous poem points out:

Happiness is something we create in our mind,
Not something we search for and so seldom find.
It's just waking up and beginning the day
By counting our blessings and kneeling to pray.
It's giving up thoughts that breed discontent
And accepting what comes as a gift heaven-sent.
It's giving up wishing for things we have not
And making the best of whatever we've got.

WEDNESDAY—SEPTEMBER 12.

SOMETIMES I like nothing better than to sit relaxing and watching television. Isn't it marvellous that from your armchair you can see so much of the world.

To many an elderly person, television is more than just pictures, voices and music. I remember reading about one lady who said that she never felt lonely with her television set. She said that, to her, the voices and faces were friends and she felt that she was never alone. It was as if the people on her small screen entered her home and kept her company.

Some people would say that our young generation watches too much television sometimes, as it distracts them from important things like homework, but to older people television is often a godsend. It brings companionship into many homes and brightens many lives.

THURSDAY—SEPTEMBER 13.

OUR church decided to hold a bread-and-water lunch, the money usually spent by the congregation on a full meal to be given to help the starving overseas. At first, though, I had some doubts. Gladly I would give money, but what was the point of such a luncheon?

"It's the sharing together," I was told, and it reminded me of an allegorical story about sharing which I once heard. A man had a dream, and in his dream he visited hell. The people there sat at a table full of food, and each had a spoon two metres long. The spoons were so long the people couldn't get any food into their mouths.

Then he visited heaven, and there the people also sat at a table full of food, and had spoons two metres long as well. But instead of trying to feed just themselves, they had learned to feed each other with these long spoons.

I went to that bread-and-water lunch, and everyone had a great deal to share.

FRIDAY—SEPTEMBER 14.

HENRY WARD BEECHER, the American preacher and writer, wrote a delightful Beatitude which seems well worth adding to the scriptural eight listed by St Matthew at the beginning of the Sermon on the Mount:

"Blessed are the happiness-makers; blessed are they who know how to shine on one's gloom with their cheer."

THE FRIENDSHIP BOOK

SATURDAY—SEPTEMBER 15.

HERE are some meaningful words from the pen of the American writer Walter MacPeck: "I believe this is a good world and that I can help to make it better. I look upon life as an adventure to be faced with eagerness. I believe in the thoughtfulness, the friendliness, the courtesy, and the cleanliness of people around me.

"When they fail to live at their best, this is merely a challenge to my leadership and the time for me to use my skill in working to make our world a better and a friendlier place."

SUNDAY—SEPTEMBER 16.

NOW the Lord of peace himself give you peace always by all means. The Lord be with you all.
Thessalonians II 3:16

MONDAY—SEPTEMBER 17.

TALK kindly to the next person you meet, and the end results can be beyond your dreams. I think the idea is neatly reflected in this verse:

Drop a pebble in the water; just a splash, and it
is gone,
But there's half-a-hundred ripples circling on and
on and on,
Kindness spreading from the centre, flowing on and
out to the sea,
And there's no sure way of telling where the end
is going to be.

TUESDAY—SEPTEMBER 18.

FACING the world with both a cheerful and courageous outlook has much to commend it, and here are a couple of thoughts for today:

The most important things in life are not things.

Don't use time or words carelessly. Neither can be retrieved.

WEDNESDAY—SEPTEMBER 19.

I ONCE stood admiring a beautifully-illustrated copy of the Lord's Prayer in a bookshop window. It held a prominent place among the display, and evoked memories of the inspired work of monks of old.

The lady standing next to me remarked, "One time we rented a holiday cottage in Snowdonia, at a beautiful spot by the river. Our son Peter was still at school at the time. One morning he suddenly just stared at the river view and over to the mountains beyond.

"That's the glory," he said. "I can't see the kingdom and the power, but I'm looking at the glory, aren't I?"

A lovely story which tells how Peter had grasped a truth that could help us all — for indeed we can see God in the beauty of the world. We can see His glory all around us in the wonder of creation, and so be led to trust in God's power and in the assurance of His kingdom upon earth.

THURSDAY—SEPTEMBER 20.

WATCHING a professional performer, it may be difficult to realise that he or she was once a novice. This applies to many skills — preaching, for example.

In his younger days John Wesley once made his way to the pulpit, only to find he had forgotten his sermon notes. Nervous and upset, he made for the vestry. An elderly woman asked him what was wrong. "Is that all?" she asked when she heard. "Can't you trust God for a sermon?" Wesley went back and preached with such vigour that he never again took a written manuscript into a pulpit.

I am reminded of a young friend who was training for the church. I asked him if he found the prospect of giving sermons daunting.

"Not at all, Francis," he replied, "I've learned the truth in the adage, 'Open your mouth, and the Lord will fill it!' "

Nothing beats confidence and trust.

FRIDAY—SEPTEMBER 21.

WORD PROCESSING

LIFE is full of do's and don'ts,
Of can and can't, of wills and won'ts,
The thing to do in all events
Is use a little commonsense.
Do your best — don't help a plan
That says you can't, although you can.
Demonstrate determined skill —
Don't say you won't, insist you will.

J.M. Robertson

SATURDAY—SEPTEMBER 22.

"SEPTEMBER blow soft till the fruit's in the loft." I thought of that old saying when I came indoors one afternoon from a sunny garden, having picked and stored the last of our apples. I found the Lady of the House putting away her newly-made pots of plum jam and apple jelly.

"Finished, Francis?" she asked. As I nodded, these lines by the poet Longfellow came to mind:

Oh, what a glory doth this world put on
For him how, with a fervent heart goes forth
Under the bright and glorious sky, and looks
On duties well performed, and days well spent!

Simple lines, but aren't they true? Doing your best on all occasions certainly does bring its own satisfaction and rewards. By the way, the Lady of the House and I later awarded ourselves a day in the country for "duties well performed", and the Autumn colours were glorious.

SUNDAY—SEPTEMBER 23.

BLESSED are the poor in spirit: for theirs is the Kingdom of Heaven.

Matthew 5: 3

MONDAY—SEPTEMBER 24.

A VERY busy executive who works in a high-tech office was asked what he regarded as his most vital piece of equipment. His answer surprised everyone.

"A paper clip," he said promptly. "It holds everything together."

TUESDAY—SEPTEMBER 25.

"IT worked, Francis," announced the voice of Neil on the phone.

"What did?" I asked, puzzled.

"Why, your advice about gardening and our new neighbours," he replied. "Don't you recall? I told you how reserved, almost standoffish they seemed, not a bit friendly, and you said . . ."

Then I remembered that I'd advised him to try a "share a plant" scheme. "It's usually a good recipe for friendship," I'd said.

"Well, one morning we met near my garden gate," Neil told me, "and I asked if they would like some cuttings from my lavender, and the rosemary bush — a notoriously difficult herb to grow in some places. As it grows so well in my garden, it is ideal for next door which has the same soil. My, you should have seen the change of attitude — it happened right away."

There are times when we should take the initiative, not just sit back and wait for others to do so. The longer you wait, the more difficult it becomes to bridge that gap.

WEDNESDAY—SEPTEMBER 26.

WE can't win all the time and sometimes, in fact, it's good to fail. It was Samuel Smiles, the social reformer, who said that we could learn more from failure than from success. He gave us this encouraging thought: "He who never made a mistake never made a discovery."

THE FRIENDSHIP BOOK

THURSDAY—SEPTEMBER 27.

HARRY and Clive were friends at school. They had a hard upbringing for they lived in a tough part of town, and their parents had a struggle making ends meet. It says a lot for them that the two boys carved out successful careers.

Harry worked his way up the ladder in industry and is now the managing director of a famous company, while Clive owns a chain of hotels.

There, sadly, the similarity ends. For while Harry has never lost touch with his parents and his home town, Clive very quickly cut himself off. His parents, now in an old folk's home, never hear from him. Clive conceals his humble origins, like a guilty secret.

Harry, on the other hand, talks proudly of all his mother and father did for him. He goes to see them as often as he can, and they want for nothing. He gives generously to his old school and is an inspiration to the pupils of today.

One of these men is happy and fulfilled. The other is not. I don't need to tell you which is the one who walks tall with a song in his heart.

FRIDAY—SEPTEMBER 28.

THE writer R. L. Stevenson, who endured so much illness in his life, wrote this personal prayer:

"Give us grace and strength to persevere. Give us courage and gaiety and the quiet mind. Spare to us our friends and soften to us our enemies".

A good recipe for a good life.

SATURDAY—SEPTEMBER 29.

I'D like to share this thought-provoking poem with you today:

DON'T RESIST

Accept the things that come your way,
*   Don't fight them, or you'll find*
That they'll get worse and out of hand,
*   As tension fills your mind.*

Accept but first ask God's advice,
*   Ask Him to share your task,*
You'll find support, right answers, strength,
*   The moment that you ask.*

Accept, don't ask, "Why should this be?"
*   Each happening is a test,*
For life on earth's a place to learn
*   The way to live the best.*

Accept the sorrows and the pain,
*   For through them we progress,*
They'll lead to patience, courage, trust,
*   And inner happiness.*

Chrissy Greenslade.

SUNDAY—SEPTEMBER 30.

LET the words of my mouth, and the meditation of my heart, be acceptable in thy sight, O Lord, my strength and my redeemer.

Psalms 19:14

October

MIDSUMMER past, the days reach out
Towards the Autumn glow
Of golden corn and falling leaves
That lead to Winter's snow.
So let us grasp the precious hours
While the season lingers on,
And keep the sunshine in our hearts
Long after Summer's gone.

Ann Rutherford.

"WHEN I look into the mirror I realise that I'm getting older," a friend once told me, "but inside I feel just the same as when I was twenty-one."

The writer J. B. Priestley who died in 1984 aged ninety, said much the same thing when he was asked what it was like to be old. "It is as though while walking down Shaftesbury Avenue as a fairly young man I was suddenly kidnapped, rushed into a theatre and made to don the grey hair, the wrinkles and other attributes of age, then wheeled on stage. Behind the facade I am the same person with the same thoughts as when I was younger," he replied.

THE FRIENDSHIP BOOK

WEDNESDAY—OCTOBER 3.

JOHN WILLIAMS was a good employer, a seasoned boot and shoe salesman who knew the wisdom and value of sensitive tactics. Claude was a somewhat brash young employee who was used to speaking the truth without stopping to think how it might sound to a customer.

It was John Williams who taught him the art of sympathetic commiseration. "I'm sorry, ma'am, but this shoe is just a little too small for your foot!"

The same facts, but different words — and what a world of difference they make!

THURSDAY—OCTOBER 4.

ONE October a mother and father were walking with their two children on the Wrekin, a hill in Shropshire. A gentle breeze was causing the Autumn leaves to fall.

One of the children stood still, her face towards the sky and her eyes closed.

"What are you doing?" her father asked.

"If a falling leaf brushes your cheek it means that you're going to be lucky," his daughter replied.

"I'll try it," he said. So he stood still, looked up and closed his eyes. Several falling leaves brushed against his cheek. He opened his eyes and looked around. He caught sight of the beauty of the countryside, the blue sky, some small drifting clouds and his wife, son and daughter.

"It works!" he said.

THE FRIENDSHIP BOOK

FRIDAY—OCTOBER 5.

IN 1927 an American housewife had an accident which meant a lengthy convalescence. To pass the long days she read books from the local library but soon she had read all the ones that interested her. What was she going to do?

"Why don't you write one yourself?" suggested her husband.

She did. "Gone With The Wind" became a bestseller, later made into one of the most popular of all films. Margaret Mitchell never stopped being grateful to her husband for his suggestion!

SATURDAY—OCTOBER 6.

A PRAYER FOR AUTUMN

DEAR Lord of all Gentleness,
Draw near to me in the Autumn of
the year.
As leaves begin to fall,
Let me remember the glories of harvest time,
The crops in the fields,
The fruit on the trees.
Teach me to share the harvest of Your love
With those I meet each day.
Let the golden beauty of this season
Remain in my life and in my heart — always.

Iris Hesselden.

SUNDAY—OCTOBER 7.

CAN any hide himself in secret places that I shall not see him? saith the Lord. Do not I fill heaven and earth? saith the Lord. Jeremiah 23:24

MONDAY—OCTOBER 8.

WHEN a local glassworks was taken over by a larger organisation, the small factory was closed down and the workers lost their jobs. They were devastated, yet didn't lose heart.

Using their redundancy money and skills acquired over the years, four former employees set up their own business in a disused workshop. Before long, they were producing fine-quality cut glass lead crystal, made and sold on the premises. All the families cooperated in the venture and those with no experience of glassmaking helped to clean and polish the finished product, serve customers in the sales area and to pack up glassware for postal delivery.

Now this industrious team is tasting the fruits of success with a thriving business, an expanded workforce and the satisfaction of good craftsmanship. As Shakespeare wrote: "There is a tide in the affairs of men, which, taken at the flood, leads on to fortune."

TUESDAY—OCTOBER 9.

AN old lady, Janet, left me a notebook in which she had jotted down many thoughts and sayings. Here are just four to share today:

"One cheer is better than a dozen groans".

"Jumping to conclusions is the worst kind of exercise".

"The best way out of any difficulty is through it".

"Those who scatter sunshine cannot live in shadow".

THE FRIENDSHIP BOOK

WEDNESDAY—OCTOBER 10.

"OH, the comfort of feeling safe with a person having neither to weigh thoughts nor measure words, but to pour them all out just as they are, chaff and grain together, knowing that a faithful hand will take and sift them, keep what is worth keeping and then, with the breath of kindness, blow the rest away."

I have known those words for many years. They were written by the 19th-century writer George Eliot — Mary Ann Evans. Born in Warwickshire, she was the author of the well-loved classics "Scenes From Clerical Life", "The Mill On The Floss" and "Silas Marner".

Aren't her words a lovely definition of understanding love and friendship? Two things to treasure above all as we journey through life.

THURSDAY—OCTOBER 11.

I ALWAYS admire the sensible thinking of people like Margaret, who lives in a cottage on the Yorkshire moors. She told me that her way of living has been influenced ever since her twenty-first birthday when her grandmother passed on to her these tips for living:

"Never run through life so fast that you forget not only where you've been, but also where you are going."

"Remember that life is not a race — it is a journey to be savoured each step of the way."

Wise words from a lady who knew the secret of contented living.

**TURNING OVER
AN OLD LEAF**

FRIDAY—OCTOBER 12.

THREE-YEAR-OLD Ian had been sick during the night, and looked very delicate by the morning. His parents felt tired the next day, but got on with life as usual.

At lunchtime Ian's grandparents arrived. There would be no chance of going to the park, as they usually did, and certainly no sweets and no ice-cream. Grandad helped with the shopping, while Grandma and Ian shared a picture book.

That evening, Ian's grandparents phoned to see how he was feeling.

They were told that when his father came home, he had asked his son if he was better.

"Yes, thank you," came the reply, "and we've had a lovely day!"

Next time we are feeling a bit under the weather, let us remember that, in spite of everything, it is still a lovely day — especially if we can share it with someone we care for and someone who cares for us.

SATURDAY—OCTOBER 13.

ARE you feeling a little bit "down" today? Then here are some words from Robert Schuller which might help:
"Tough times never last;
Tough people do."

SUNDAY—OCTOBER 14.

AND Jesus said unto him, Receive thy sight: thy faith hath saved thee.   Luke 18:42

MONDAY—OCTOBER 15.

WHEN things start to go wrong and it seems that everything is against you, keep in mind these words written some years ago by Loretta Girzartis.

"If someone listens, or stretches out a hand, or whispers a kind word of encouragement, or attempts to understand a lonely person, then extraordinary things begin to happen."

And happen they do, as I have discovered. Extraordinary things, thanks to ordinary people.

TUESDAY—OCTOBER 16.

A VICAR asked his congregation, "Do you remember when biscuits weren't pre-packed? You chose those you wanted from tins, and they were weighed out for you. Broken biscuits were separated out and sold cheaply.

"With a selection of broken biscuits you could put your hand into the bag and pick out pieces at random, so each mouthful was a surprise and a delight."

He then picked up a biscuit from a plate on the ledge of the pulpit, held it up and broke off a piece. "We're all rather like broken biscuits. Deep down we've all been a little broken, perhaps by disappointment, bereavement, pain or loneliness.

"Now, don't leave the jobs that need doing in this church or anywhere else to those lucky people who are completely unbroken. You see, there aren't any! Last but not least — I hope you can stay for tea and biscuits after the service!"

THE FRIENDSHIP BOOK

WEDNESDAY—OCTOBER 17.

HOW refreshing it is to read Hannah Hauxwell's books. The enchanting lady from Barnsdale, who endured such hardships for many years on her hill-top farm, then travelled widely all over the world to meet like minded people of many nations.

In "Hannah In America" we meet the Amish people who make their home in Lancaster County, Pennsylvania.

"You go back in time when meeting them and seeing the way they live and work," says Hannah, "with no mod cons, no electricity in the home or on the farm." A life, not unlike Hannah's was, until comparatively recent times.

They have a simple philosophy of life that we could all learn from. They hold fast to their traditional customs and beliefs, work long hours, and have a tremendous community spirit, helping and working for each other.

Hannah felt very proud to have met the Amish people and admired their principles. Now, I think there are a lot of us who feel the same way about Hannah Hauxwell, don't you?

THURSDAY—OCTOBER 18.

WHEN the night is dark, reach out for a star,
When life turns against you, reach out
for hope,
When sadness surrounds you, reach out
for love,
And always, always, reach out for your dreams.

FRIDAY—OCTOBER 19.

THE Lady of the House and I were talking one day about our circle of friends, and saying a quiet thank-you for the fact that, over the years, we have gathered a fair number of them. They are in all age groups and can be found in many parts of the world. Which qualities, we mused, really make a friend?

Friends, we finally decided, are a very rare jewel. They are the sort of people who make you smile, the kind who encourage you to succeed. They are the people who always lend an ear, who share a word of praise, and who are always on hand to open their hearts to you.

SATURDAY—OCTOBER 20.

I WAS thumbing through a magazine one day when I came across this quotation:

"When you love someone, draw a circle around their name instead of a heart, because hearts can be broken but circles never end."

I liked the thought so much that I drew a circle round the words so that I would remember to pass them on.

SUNDAY—OCTOBER 21.

AND ye my flock, the flock of my pasture, are men, and I am your God, saith the Lord God.

Ezekiel 34:31

THE FRIENDSHIP BOOK

<u>MONDAY—OCTOBER 22.</u>

TODAY is precious, so handle with loving care — tomorrow you will remember only the sunshine.

<u>TUESDAY—OCTOBER 23.</u>

CHILDREN'S questions need to be answered for you never know just what lies behind them. Of course, it's not always easy to answer convincingly, but Joanne's mother made a real effort when her daughter asked: "Mummy, do you love me?"

"Of course," replied her mother.

"But how much?" persisted Joanne.

"With all my heart," her mother said, smiling gently.

But Joanne wasn't satisfied even then. "Yes, but if you love me with all your heart, what about Colin and Daddy? Your heart can't be big enough for all that loving, and for Grandma and Grandpa and . . ."

"Oh, yes, it can," interrupted her mother gently. "You see, darling, it doesn't matter whether the heart is big or little — all that matters is how much love there is — there's lots and lots of love in mine, and it overflows just like water overflows if you leave the tap turned on.

"Now, you can turn a tap off and stop the water flowing but you can't ever turn off the love in my heart."

Joanne gave a beaming smile. She had been reassured.

WEDNESDAY—OCTOBER 24.

I LIKE the story of a 10-year-old boy who was very interested in cars and made a study of their different makes and models. When he noticed a shining Rolls-Royce parked outside, he couldn't resist going closer. When its owner returned, he found the lad staring intently through the window.

The lad explained his great interest in cars, then surprised the owner by telling him a lot of details about his car. Then the boy asked, "Excuse me, sir, but how much did you pay for this car?"

The owner replied: "Nothing — my brother gave it to me."

The boy responded, "I wish . . ." and then stopped.

The man laughed. "You were going to say, 'I wish I had a brother like that!' weren't you?"

"No — I was going to say 'I wish I could *be* a brother like that.' I have a brother who is not at all well, and I'd like to do a lot of things to help him."

A marvellous illustration of the spirit of giving rather than the spirit of getting, don't you think?

THURSDAY—OCTOBER 25.

THERE are no clues as to who originally uttered these words, but I think they are well worth sharing:

"You don't stop laughing because you grow old. You grow old because you stop laughing."

FRIDAY—OCTOBER 26.

SOMETIMES, with luck, we find the kind of true friend, male or female, that appears only two or three times in a lucky lifetime, one that will Winter us and Summer us, grieve, rejoice and travel with us.

Barbara Holland.

SATURDAY—OCTOBER 27.

THE famous artist J. M. W. Turner owed much encouragement and help to Walter Fawkes of Farnley Hall, Wharfedale, in West Yorkshire. He was determined to portray the beauty of our country in sketches and paintings.

After his early visits to Yorkshire, Walter Fawkes invited him to make Farnley Hall his base, and from 1797 until 1824 (when his friend died) Turner set out from Wharfedale on lengthy and often difficult journeys through the north of England and farther afield.

As he had a comfortable base Turner was able to explore the countryside and reveal its delights in pictures. Probably Fawkes never imagined his hospitality would have such a lasting effect on British art. Yet it undoubtedly did.

We never know just how far-reaching our helpful actions to others along the way can be.

SUNDAY—OCTOBER 28.

CHARITY suffereth long, and is kind; charity envieth not; charity vaunteth not itself, is not puffed up.
Corinthians I 13:4

THE FRIENDSHIP BOOK

MONDAY—OCTOBER 29.

MOTHER TERESA was adored throughout the world, and her thoughts and teaching continue to inspire. She once said:

"Kind thoughts can be short and easy to speak, but their echoes are endless."

TUESDAY—OCTOBER 30.

I 'M making a report on me,
*   Just like the ones at school,*
And straight away, it's plain to see
*   I've broken every rule.*
They said, "You must try harder"
*   And "Could do better", too,*
Then "Shouldn't talk so much,"
*   And "Pay attention — do!"*
Well, now those days are far away
*   But still my faults appear,*
I try so hard to concentrate,
*   Improving year by year.*
So, in that end-of-term report
*   Beyond the last great test,*
I hope the Master's comments read:
*   "Well done! You did your best!"*
Iris Hesselden.

WEDNESDAY—OCTOBER 31.

ON days when none of your clouds seem to have a silver lining, it is worth remembering those wise words of Dr Samuel Johnson:

"It is worth a thousand pounds a year to have the habit of looking on the bright side of things."

November

<u>THURSDAY—NOVEMBER 1.</u>

A GROUP of primary school pupils were asked by their teacher to record some personal thoughts on their parents. Ten-year-old Hannah wrote: "Always remember, you are never too old to hold your father's hand."

<u>FRIDAY—NOVEMBER 2.</u>

THE little Summer of St Martin can be a jewel in the crown of November, when real Winter is just around the corner, a brief succession of sweet, mild days, calm and sunny, with blue skies, when it may be warm enough to sit out in a sheltered spot in the garden.

Now, I wonder if you have heard the story of St Martin? It is said that when he died, the boat which carried his body up river had neither oar nor sail, and although it was late in the year, it seemed like Summer once more — flowers bloomed and leaves were green again on the river banks.

Sometimes these days of sweet tranquillity are called an Indian Summer, but whatever we call these fleeting days of mild, blue skies, they leave a sunny memory of November which is pleasant to recall on colder Winter days.

SATURDAY—NOVEMBER 3.

I WAS out last week when I happened to overhear a young man quip rather wryly to his friend, "Life is something that happens to you while you're waiting for it to get going."

The remark made me smile, for isn't it true? So many of us are content to spend our days just marking time, waiting for something to happen to change us or to alter the world in which we live. By the time we've decided which direction we would like to take, it is sometimes, sadly, too late to make the choice.

So next time I'm tempted to put off decisions, and simply wait for events to overtake me, I shall try to remember that young man's remark. I may have passed the stage of waiting for life to get started, but there's no reason why I shouldn't have some say in which direction it goes!

SUNDAY—NOVEMBER 4.

AND the disciples were filled with joy, and with the Holy Ghost.

Acts 13: 52

MONDAY—NOVEMBER 5.

I RECEIVED a letter one morning from a friend who knows how much I like to collect memorable sayings. This quote which he passed on is from the pen of Ralph Waldo Emerson and gives much food for thought:

"It is one of the most beautiful compensations of life, that no man can sincerely try to help another without helping himself."

THE FRIENDSHIP BOOK

TUESDAY—NOVEMBER 6.

OUR street lamp hadn't been working for several days and we really missed its light — a typical example of the many things which we take for granted nowadays. In the centuries when our great cathedrals were being built, people's lives were ruled by when the sun rose and set. Any extra light and colour from other sources was more than welcome.

The beautiful stained glass windows provided worshippers with extra light and they also depicted Bible stories beautifully. This was also a way people could learn visually.

When visiting York I love to look at the rose window in the Minster, created all those decades ago with such love and dedication.

Once our street lamp was repaired, it brought light into our lives once more, just as Jesus, the Light of the World, did.

WEDNESDAY—NOVEMBER 7.

IT is always wise to build up friendships gradually, though we shouldn't be put off striking up a good acquaintanceship whenever the right opportunity comes along. That's the very advice which I once read in a church magazine:

"Yesterday I met a stranger. Today that stranger is my friend. Now, had I not taken the time to say hello, or return a smile, I would not have known this person. Yesterday would have turned into today and our chance meeting would be gone."

POPPY DAY

THE FRIENDSHIP BOOK

THURSDAY—NOVEMBER 8.

WE were once at a wedding, and were looking forward to hearing the speeches at the reception afterwards. The best man received early bursts of applause as he treated the guests to some ten minutes of wise and witty thoughts about love, life and marriage.

But we gave a big hand, too, to an absolute gem of a quotation delivered by the father of the bride as he wished his daughter and son-in-law happiness in their life together. We didn't catch the name of the author of the quotation he delivered but the words, I feel, are well worth sharing today:

"May the roof over your head never fall in, and the friends gathered below never fall out."

FRIDAY—NOVEMBER 9.

STROLLING home one evening I met a neigh bour, Nicola, walking along and holding her little boy's hand. David was crying.

When I asked what was wrong, Nicola replied that David wanted the moon, thinking it was a balloon rising into the sky. It was little wonder he was so captivated — the moon was a brilliant sight that evening, its light transforming every cloud into silver.

Standing beside young David, I, too, felt that same sense of wonder, an example of nature which has inspired man for centuries:

"Unto Thee lift I up mine eyes o Thou that dwellest in the heavens."

SATURDAY—NOVEMBER 10.

SOMEONE once said: "Let us be contented with all that has happened to us and thankful for all we have been spared."

I thought of these words when I heard two people complaining about their problems. I wanted to interrupt and ask them about the good times. Ask them if they had ever been homeless, seriously ill or unloved. But I happened to know that none of these things applied and I felt they were being rather ungrateful, even though it is undoubtedly true that we all have off days when nothing seems right.

Let us try to aim for contentment with our lot and be especially thankful for all that we have been spared.

SUNDAY—NOVEMBER 11.

BUT now, O Lord, thou art our father; we are the clay, and thou our potter; and we all are the work of thy hand.

Isaiah 64:8

MONDAY—NOVEMBER 12.

IT is good to set our sights on achieving, no matter how difficult the project may at first appear. The words of President John F. Kennedy fit that goal perfectly: "Only those who dare to fail greatly can achieve greatly."

It's a thought that is well worth remembering. Keep it in mind today.

TUESDAY—NOVEMBER 13.

ONE of our neighbours, Eric, came back from a visit to the United States recently and kept extending the wish to all of us to "Have a nice day!" This has become the favourite phrase of Americans as they say their temporary good-byes in business and leisure. It has caught on as an expression of goodwill throughout the world.

Our friend's use of the phrase made me think of all the other favourite expressions of good wishes and friendship that have been used over the years — for instance, "Be seeing you!" or "Cheerio!" There are many others, of course, such as the much-heard "Take care" or "Mind how you go."

I'm sure it all adds up to a simple expression of good wishes for the rest of each day and of general friendliness. There can be no better goal than that, surely.

WEDNESDAY—NOVEMBER 14.

*RAIN upon the pavement, rain upon
the street,
Filling up the puddles, drenching careless feet.
Bouncing off the tarmac, splashing on the doors,
Dripping off the awnings — goodness, how
it pours!
Safe behind my window, watching people pass,
I see the Wintry raindrops beating on the glass.
Now I close the curtains, get the hearth-fire lit —
There are a few occasions when I don't mind
rain one bit!*
Margaret Ingall.

THURSDAY—NOVEMBER 15.

WHAT a wealth of wisdom can be found in a few words! Here are some of my favourite sayings to share with you today:

"A friend is the one who comes in when the whole world has gone out."

"Eat well, sleep deeply. Tomorrow comes and it is all yours."

And this one, from Holland, encourages us when we are hesitant: "He who is outside his door already has a hard part of his journey behind him."

FRIDAY—NOVEMBER 16.

THERE is something very pleasant and comfortable about sitting indoors, relaxing after all the to-ing and fro-ing of a busy day. By that time, I've read the newspapers, listened to the weather forecast and, as the clock strikes eleven, I like to dip into a favourite anthology. One evening I saw these lines by Charles Kingsley, the author of "Westward Ho" and "The Water Babies":

The world goes up and the world goes down,
And the sunshine follows the rain;
And yesterday's sneer and yesterday's frown
Can never come over again,
Sweet wife;
No, never come over again.

Surely wise, comforting words to reflect on, when we experience unhappy days in our life, as all of us do at some time or another.

THE FRIENDSHIP BOOK

SATURDAY—NOVEMBER 17.

I WAS interested to read about a vicar in one of our northern cities who offered a free home and a nominal salary to a family willing to give a friendly smile to fellow residents on a troubled housing estate.

Qualifications and experience were not necessary in this Good Neighbour scheme to help combat crime and low morale on the estate. What was being looked for was the ability to set a cheerful example and provide a friendly place for people to get together for a chat, or perhaps seek advice. It's a new angle on "love thy neighbour" and hugely worthwhile.

SUNDAY—NOVEMBER 18.

I WILL call on the Lord, who is worthy to be praised: so shall I be saved from mine enemies.
Samuel II 22:4

MONDAY—NOVEMBER 19.

OUR friend Margaret had thought of several things she might give her mother for her birthday, but none seemed just right. How she heaved a sigh of relief when her mother told her that what she needed was a new garden fork.

"Mine is on its last legs, so a new one will come in handy for planting the Spring vegetables, and I might try a different variety of early potato this year as well."

Now that's what I call positive thinking from a keen gardener, celebrating her 91st birthday!

TUESDAY—NOVEMBER 20.

ONCE more the firm's annual dinner had come to an end. The employees had dined well, listened to the chairman's speech and had met several old acquaintances. Later, everyone said their farewells in the hotel foyer but when they stepped outside they discovered, to their dismay, that dense fog had descended.

As everyone contemplated the hazards of getting home, telephonist Bert appeared.

"What's up?" he asked.

"Pea souper," came the reply. "Nothing's moving — no buses, no taxis."

"Not to worry," said Bert, grinning. "We'll walk. Just follow me, I'll get you home."

And so he did — fog presented no problems for Bert. He was blind.

WEDNESDAY—NOVEMBER 21.

I WOULD like to share with you these wise words seen on the notice-board of a little village church:

Life is about who you love and who you hurt.
It's about who you make happy or unhappy.
It's about keeping, not betraying trust.
It's about friendship.
It's about what you say and mean.
It's about stopping jealousy, fear,
    ignorance and revenge.
But most of all, it's about using your life to touch another person's heart in such a way that could never have occurred alone.

THE FRIENDSHIP BOOK

WHEN the children's writer J.K. Rowling was working on her first book she could not afford to heat her tiny Edinburgh flat. Every day she went to a restaurant where the staff let her sit and write at a quiet table. Sometimes they slipped her a free cup of coffee.

No-one was more delighted than the staff there when the book she'd been writing, "Harry Potter And The Philosopher's Stone", became an instant bestseller. "Their kindness to me made all the difference," she said.

THANK You, Lord, for the good times,
The happiness and fun,
The days of laughing in the rain,
Or lazing in the sun.
The times of looking forward
With not a care in sight,
The days when all our plans and schemes
Could set the world alight.

And even when the doubts and fears
Came knocking on our door,
We faced them all, with help from You,
And learned to smile once more.
The years were far too precious
To waste or to regret,
So thank You, Lord, for the good times,
I never will forget!

Iris Hesselden.

SATURDAY—NOVEMBER 24.

A GOOD friend of ours, Violet, found this verse below a photograph on a calendar and I'd like to share it with you today:

I watch the sparrow in the snow,
Its dainty footsteps come and go,
As it invites us to recall
A chirpy nature's best of all,
Which, in its way, can offer crumbs
Of comfort when harsh Winter comes.

SUNDAY—NOVEMBER 25.

A ND Jesus said unto them, I am the bread of life: he that cometh to me shall never hunger: and he that believeth on me shall never thirst.   John 6: 35

MONDAY—NOVEMBER 26.

I T was a dreadful day — cold, windy and with torrential rain. A taxi driver was having a busy afternoon taking shoppers home from the town centre. Having dropped off one passenger safely in the middle of a large residential estate, he turned a corner and had quite a surprise.

Walking sedately down the middle of the road was a pair of mallards — duck and drake, side by side — in the pouring rain! Where they came from and where they later went is a mystery, but they certainly gave the driver a smile he badly needed. As he said to us later, it gave a whole new meaning to that expression: "Lovely weather for ducks!"

THESE ARE MY MOUNTAINS

TUESDAY—NOVEMBER 27.

LORRAINE had to work late at the library. It had been a long, tiring day and it was dark and cold as she made her way home. Her young son John greeted her at the door and took her through to the kitchen where his father was cooking supper. Then Lorraine was led upstairs to the bathroom where a warm, perfumed bath was waiting.

As she remarked to us the next day, "It's so nice to be pampered now and then."

Perhaps you know someone who might like a little pampering today. I'm sure that they will feel much better for it and, when you see their pleasure and surprise, so will you!

WEDNESDAY—NOVEMBER 28.

HERE are a few words for us to consider when we start worrying about trivia:

"Please don't worry about the world coming to an end today. It is already a bright tomorrow here in Australia."

These words were spoken to me on the phone by our friend Margaret in Brisbane. We all know that there is a time difference between us and Australia, but how many of us remember that a bright new day will have dawned "Down Under" when it's dark and approaching midnight in this country?

The sun is always shining brightly somewhere in the world.

THURSDAY—NOVEMBER 29.

SUNDAY school was in session in a Yorkshire town. The classes were separated only by partitions which went barely halfway up the room. The teacher of one class became annoyed beyond endurance by the noisy behaviour of boys nearby.

He walked round the partition, glared at the biggest boy who seemed to be making the most noise, and ushered him over into his own class, telling him to sit in the corner and behave.

For a few moments, there was an almost unearthly silence and then a small voice piped up: "Please, sir, you've taken our teacher!"

FRIDAY—NOVEMBER 30.

ONE bleak Winter's day when frost lay thick on the ground, how I longed for the green leaves and scented flowers of Summer! It seemed that the countryside was devoid of all beauty and colour.

But later, when I went to visit our old friend Mary, she led me towards her kitchen window. A holly tree was to be seen a few feet away.

"Look," she said, "isn't that a lovely sight?"

There, feeding on the red berries, bright against the dark green leaves, was a flock of redwings. They are so named because of the red plumage under their wings. I thought of these words:

Even in the darkest days,
In sky, on branch and ground,
God's wonders never cease
His beauty ever found.

December

THOUGHTS

*S*END *out your loving, caring thoughts*
On gentle, healing wings,
So they may travel far and wide,
For thoughts are living things.

Send out your thoughts to those you know
And those for whom you care,
To those in trouble or distress,
In sickness or despair.

And send your thoughts around the earth
To each far distant shore,
Till children of the world unite
And fight and war no more.

For loving thoughts create a peace
And joy which can't be bought,
So never underestimate
The power of your thought.

Iris Hesselden.

AND God said, Let there be light: and there was light.

Genesis 1: 3

THE FRIENDSHIP BOOK

MONDAY—DECEMBER 3.

YOUNG Stephen's mother thought that having two sets of grandparents might make life complicated for him as he grew older, but it didn't. The ladies decided to be Nanna and Grandma, and the two men both chose Grandad. By the time Stephen could talk, he referred to "Nanna's Grandad" and "Grandma's Grandad." Obviously, it was quite straightforward to him.

The family became used to these descriptions and took them for granted. But the day came when everyone had a good laugh, though not unkindly, at the little boy's expense. Stephen had started nursery school, and on this particular day made straight for his teacher.

"Mrs Brown," he shouted excitedly, "Do you know, it's Grandma's Grandad's birthday today!"

"Really?" replied the teacher, slightly taken aback. "Well, he must be very old."

As Stephen already thought Grandad was very old, this didn't bother him one bit. He went off happily to do a painting as a birthday gift.

TUESDAY—DECEMBER 4.

HERE'S a well-known saying to keep in mind during the dark days of Winter: "God gave us memory, that we might have roses in December."

When days are short and the weather distinctly chilly, think of happy times and bring sunshine to your Winter skies.

WEDNESDAY—DECEMBER 5.

MANY years ago a young mother, carrying her baby in her arms, was making her way across the hills of south Wales when she was caught in a blizzard. She never reached her destination and, when the storm had subsided, her body was found in a mound of snow.

Searchers feared that her baby would have perished as well but, before she died, the mother had taken off all her outer clothing to wrap up the child. They found him alive and well. The child's name was David Lloyd George and he grew up to become Prime Minister of Great Britain, one of our great statesmen.

Today I would like to take time to think of all mothers for their loving sacrifices. As the saying goes; "God couldn't be everywhere — that's why he created mothers".

THURSDAY—DECEMBER 6.

MARTIN is one of these practical folk who moves swiftly when a difficult job has to be completed.

"I adopt this attitude whenever life seems dark and dreary," he says. "Apply it to the art of being happy, as well. We should all go out and make our own happiness and stop waiting for something or someone to make us happy. There is no better time than right now to be happy."

The smile on Martin's face proves how happy he is with his life and work.

FRIDAY—DECEMBER 7.

HERE is a saying which I'd like to share with you:

Look well to this day — it is one of a kind and will never come again.

SATURDAY—DECEMBER 8.

ROBERT LOUIS STEVENSON is perhaps best remembered for his novels "Treasure Island" and "Kidnapped", stirring tales beloved of schoolchildren. He suffered from poor health, and once, as he lay in bed, he watched the lamplighter going round, lighting the lamps one by one. Stevenson reflected that he was "watching a man making holes in the darkness."

Now, when you stop to think, it only needs one light in the darkness to make a difference. Black holes are not completely dark if there is a light somewhere. And if there are several lights it makes even more difference.

A railway traveller tells me that he always looks forward to emerging from a particular tunnel, because the little lights he sees on coming out reassure him that he is nearly home. As the Good Book reminds us, the light always shines in the darkness, and the darkness has never been able to overcome it.

SUNDAY—DECEMBER 9.

I SAY to you, inasmuch as ye have done it unto one of the least of these my brethren, ye have done it unto me.   Matthew 25:40

ON THE BLUE
HORIZON

MONDAY—DECEMBER 10.

DIPPING into a favourite book from childhood one afternoon – "Anne Of Avonlea" by L. M. Montgomery – I came across this paragraph:

"The nicest and sweetest days are not those on which anything very splendid or wonderful or exciting happens, but just those that bring simple little pleasures, following one another softly, like pearls slipping off a string."

May your day be just such a one.

TUESDAY—DECEMBER 11.

EVER since mankind found that by hitting two sticks together a sound was produced, our lives have been dominated by music. It expresses every human emotion in its many forms.

We smile or shed tears to it, dance to its notes, and how soothing it is after a hard day's work to lie back and listen to music and feel all our stresses melt away. Music uplifts the soul and great composers have praised God in this way for centuries — to listen to an organ or choir in the splendour of a cathedral's setting is truly awe-inspiring.

One leading churchman has said: "Many a person has become a Christian just by coming to listen to evensong." As it says in Psalms 138: "They shall sing in the ways of the Lord: for great is the glory of the Lord."

It would be a poorer world without music to enrich our lives.

WEDNESDAY—DECEMBER 12.

THESE verses were written anonymously and appeared in the official publication of "The Countrywomen's Association of Victoria". Think about them next time you're busy in the kitchen preparing a meal or even washing up all the crockery afterwards.

A KITCHEN PRAYER

Lord of all pots and pans and things
Since I've no time to be
A saint by doing lovely things
Or storming Heaven's gates,
Make me a saint by getting meals
And washing up the plates.

Accept this meditation, Lord
I haven't time for more,
Light all my kitchen with Thy peace
And warm it with Thy love.
Help all earth's hunger cease
Thou who once fed men by the sea,
Accept this service that I do
For I do it unto Thee.

THURSDAY—DECEMBER 13.

"NO-ONE ever injured their eyesight by looking on the bright side of things."

Isn't it a pity that the author of such a happy sentiment is unknown to us? I'm sure you'll agree that he — or she — had exactly the right motto for living.

FRIDAY—DECEMBER 14.

PEOPLE in different parts of the world have their own way of wishing us happiness in the future. Here's a quote that the Lady of the House and I liked, sent to us by friends in the sunshine state of California:

"May you always have walls for the winds, a roof for the rain, tea beside the fire, laughter to cheer you, those you love near you, and all that your heart may desire."

SATURDAY—DECEMBER 15.

DURING an Advent service, the minister enlisted the help of a few children to explain the significance of several new banners which had been prepared for the Christmas season. One depicted the crib, with the infant Jesus, Mary and Joseph, and the cattle in the background.

"This doesn't seem a very posh hotel they're staying in," remarked the minister. "It doesn't look like a three-star or four-star one to me."

A young voice piped up, "Of course it isn't — it's a one-star!"

And when you come to think of it, that's exactly what it was!

SUNDAY—DECEMBER 16.

AND whatsoever ye do in word or deed, do all in the name of the Lord Jesus, giving thanks to God and the Father by him.
Colossians 3:17

MONDAY—DECEMBER 17.

OUR friend Lorna saw this sign in a church hall: "Remember, everyone you will meet here is afraid of something, loves something, and has lost something. Be a friend to all."

A timely reminder that a kind and friendly word can mean so much to someone.

TUESDAY—DECEMBER 18.

DURING the First World War a German doctor by the name of Gerhard Stalling taught his dog a few useful exercises, and one day noticed his pet led a blinded soldier across a hospital lawn.

This led him to set up the first recognised training of guide dogs for the blind, an idea taken up by a wealthy American animal lover called Dorothy Eustis, who began L'Œil Qui Voit in the Swiss town of Vevey in 1928. This was followed three years later by a similar movement in Wallasey on the Wirral peninsula.

It was the beginning of Guide Dogs For The Blind, a movement recognised throughout the world, which has brought to so many partially-sighted people the ability to walk almost anywhere, knowing that their faithful dog will guide them in complete safety.

WEDNESDAY—DECEMBER 19.

THE Music of Christmas is Laughter;
The Warmth of Christmas is Friendship;
And the Spirit of Christmas is Love.

IN THE PINK

THURSDAY—DECEMBER 20.

REVIEW IT

IF a ploy brings joy, pursue it.
Where there's scope for hope, renew it.

If trouble's lurking, view it,
Then start working to subdue it.

If worry's wooing, shoo it.
If a job's worth doing, do it.

J.M. Robertson.

FRIDAY—DECEMBER 21.

ONE should keep old roads and old friends.
German proverb.

SATURDAY—DECEMBER 22.

THE THREE CAMELS

ONE camel said, "I've got the hump —
This king is such a heavy lump,
I've carried him both night and day
And now I think I've lost my way."

The next one said, "Then follow me —
A shining star ahead I see,
And all will come from near and far
Led onwards by that guiding star."

"They're searching for a new-born King"
The third one said, "And Peace He'll bring.
And in a stable, so 'tis said
They'll find him in a manger bed."

Dorothy M. Loughran.

SUNDAY—DECEMBER 23.

THEREFORE the Lord himself shall give you a sign; Behold a virgin shall conceive, and bear a son, and shall call his name Immanuel.

Isaiah 7:14

MONDAY—DECEMBER 24.

T WAS the night before Christmas, when all through the house, Not a creature was stirring, not even a mouse . . .

So begins "The Night Before Christmas", probably the best-known children's Christmas poem, an evocative picture of children snug in bed awaiting the visit of St Nicholas.

The writer, perhaps surprisingly, was a professor of Oriental languages named Clement Clarke Moore. In New York just before Christmas in 1822, one of Professor Moore's small sons had been hurt in a riding accident. His had not been a serious injury, but sadly, the pony had died afterwards. The boy was inconsolable, and so the serious-minded professor sat at his desk and penned a poem in an attempt to make his unhappy little son smile again.

It did the trick, for the youngster's cheerful spirits returned. A year later, the poem was published anonymously and children and adults all over the world were captivated by its sentiments. Perhaps Professor Moore would give a wry smile to know that he is remembered today, not for academic work, but as the writer of a simple poem.

TUESDAY—DECEMBER 25.

*S*O now God bless us, one and all,
  With hearts and hearthstones warm;
And may he prosper great and small
  And keep us out of harm,
And teach us still
  His sweet goodwill
This merry Christmas morning.

Don't these lines from Edwin Waugh's Victorian poem "Christmas Morning" express the best of seasonal wishes? The Lady of the House and I send the very same Christmas greetings to you all!

Happy Christmas!

WEDNESDAY—DECEMBER 26.

*L*OOKING at the Christmas cards upon the wall, I always notice how they capture the spirit of the season so well. Some will recall that bygone world of horse-drawn carriages on snow-covered country roads, while others will portray the many outdoor beauties of this season — holly bushes coated with red berries, snowflakes clinging to pine needles, frost like tinsel on the hedgerows.

Bells, too, are a common feature for they are such an integral part of the festive season. At few other times of year do bells ring out in such unison from the steeples of the greatest cathedrals to the smallest village church. When they peal out the old and ring in the new at New Year, we sincerely hope that peace and goodwill will remain in our hearts throughout the year.

THURSDAY—DECEMBER 27.

CHARLOTTE Brontë's friend Mary Taylor was also a novelist although a less famous one. In her novel "Miss Miles" a father gives some advice to his daughter Rio:

"That of this be sure, Rio, that what will give you most pleasure when the time comes will be the good that you may have done to others. Do you understand that?"

He continued: "The time will certainly come when you may do good to someone. Then do it with all your might — always on all occasions. And remember this. When your own affairs seem past mercy, when there seems no hope of gladness in your life, try to help someone else, and light will come!"

An almost forgotten novel, but one with a modern message.

FRIDAY—DECEMBER 28.

"FOUR seasons in one day!" Hilda grumbled. "I'm fed up with this weather. This morning was misty, then it became sunny, then the rain swept in, and now it's blowing a gale! I wish we had a country where the sun shone all the time."

I knew just what she meant, but I couldn't quite agree. Permanent Summer might sound pleasant, but how sad never to experience a crisp and golden Autumn day; the stark beauty of a Winter sky, or the sight of the first Spring flowers.

And although the weather doesn't do what we want, it never manages to be boring!

SATURDAY—DECEMBER 29.

OUR friend Dora came across a brown envelope addressed to herself with a postmark eight years old. It contained a certificate in her name when she had donated a small amount to have a tree planted.

Dora realised that by then "her" tree would still be growing, just one tree amongst the many given by different people and organisations to help beautify our countryside.

Most people cannot afford to plant a forest, but combined efforts have a lasting result.

SUNDAY—DECEMBER 30.

HE maketh me to lie down in green pastures: he leadeth me beside the still waters.

Psalms 23: 2.

MONDAY—DECEMBER 31.

THE Lady of the House and I have Scottish friends who always send us a New Year card. One year, they wrote these lines inside our card and, as the year draws to a close, we think that you will appreciate sharing their sentiments:

Here's to the friends we can trust
When storms of adversity blaw;
May they live in our songs and be nearest
our hearts,
Nor depart like the year that's awa.

Those lines were written by the Scottish songwriter John Dunlop, who was born in 1755.

A happy New Year to you all!

The Photographs

WHILE SHEEP SAFELY GRAZE — *Vale of Ewyas, Cwmyoy, Powys.*
ON THE RIGHT TRACK — *The "Jacobite", leaving Glenfinnan.*
GUARDIAN OF THE GLEN — *Buachaille Etive Mor, Glen Coe.*
THE TIME OF HIS LIFE — *Dervaig, Mull.*
A GOLDEN MOMENT — *Eilean Donan Castle.*
SPRINGTIME PROMISE — *Lake Windermere, Cumbria.*
COUNTRY CALM — *Shottesbrook, Berkshire.*
STOP, LOOK AND LISTEN — *Troutbeck, Cumbria.*
SHEER BEAUTY — *Beachy Head Lighthouse, near Eastbourne.*
LEARNING THE ROPES — *Abingdon-on-Thames.*
TWO'S COMPANY — *The River Aire, Yorkshire.*
PALM, POOL AND PEACE — *Port Logan, Wigtownshire.*
GRACIOUS GABLES — *Little Moreton Hall, Cheshire.*
REFLECTED GLORY — *Sango Bay, Sutherland.*
TWICE AS NICE — *Sheffield Park Gardens, East Sussex.*
ACROSS THE MILES — *Looking north to North Middleton Village*
and Midlothian.
BRANCHING OUT — *River North Esk, Angus.*
CUT AND TIED — *Cunningsburgh, Shetland.*
THESE ARE MY MOUNTAINS — *Loch Cluanie, West Highlands.*
IN THE PINK — *Arisaig, Inverness-shire.*
WINDOW TO HEAVEN — *Dunfermline Abbey, Fife.*

ACKNOWLEDGMENTS: **Paul Felix;** While Sheep Safely Graze, Country Calm. **David Bigwood;** First Flowers, After The Rain. **A. Taylor;** Bird's Eye View. **Duncan I. McEwan;** Guardian Of The Glen, Meadowsweet, Reflected Glory, Branching Out, In The Pink. **Willie Shand;** On The Right Track, Window To Heaven. **Douglas Laidlaw;** The Time Of His Life. **Stephen and Norma Goodwin;** A Golden Moment. **Douglas Kerr;** Gentle Giants. **V.K. Guy;** Springtime Promise, Stop, Look And Listen, Cut And Tied. **Sheila Taylor;** In A Flap, Poppy Day. **Andy Williams;** Sheer Beauty, Turning Over An Old Leaf. **Ivan J. Belcher;** Learning The Ropes. **Clifford Robinson;** Two's Company. **Dennis Hardley;** Palm, Pool And Peace, Gracious Gables, Twice As Nice, These Are My Mountains. **Martin H. Moar;** Across The Miles. **Steve Austin;** On The Blue Horizon.

Printed and Published by D. C. Thomson & Co., Ltd.,
185 Fleet Street, London EC4A 2HS.
© D. C. Thomson & Co., Ltd., 2000   **ISBN** 0-85116-739-X